CONSECRATED LIFE:
A Renewed Insight

Mary Bride Njoku OSB

CONSECRATED LIFE:
A Renewed Insight

Every effort has been made to trace copyright holders and to obtain their permission for the use of copyright material. The publisher apologises for any errors or omissions in the above list and would be grateful if notified of any corrections that should be incorporated in future reprints or editions of this book.

ST PAULS by Westminster Cathedral
Morpeth Terrace, Victoria, London SW1P 1E
Ph: +44 (0)207978 4300
www.stpauls.org.uk

ST PAULS PUBLISHING
Moyglare Road, Maynooth, Co. Kildare, Ireland
Ph: +353 (1) 628 5933
www.stpauls.ie

ISBN: 978-1-910365-14-4

Layout and cover design by Middledot

Printed in Malta by Melita Press

A CIP catalogue record for this book is available from the British Library.

ST PAULS is an activity of the priests and brothers of the Society of St Paul who proclaim the Gospel through the media of social communication

CONTENTS

ABBREVIATIONS

DOCUMENTS OF THE SECOND VATICAN COUNCIL

LG Dogmatic Constitution: *Lumen Gentium*, 1965

PC Decree *Perfectae Caritatis*, 1965

DOCUMENTS OF THE POPES

EG Apostolic Exhortation *Evangelii Gaudium*, Francis, 2013

ET Apostolic Exhortation *Evangelica Testificatio*, Paul VI, 1971

PDV Apostolic Exhortation *Pastores Dabo Vobis*, John Paul II, 1992

RD Apostolic Exhortation *Redemptionis Donum*, John Paul II, 1984

VC Apostolic Exhortation *Vita Consecrata*, John Paul II, 1996

DOCUMENTS OF THE HOLY SEE

Can Canon or canons of *Codex Iuris Canonici*, 1983.

EE *Essential Elements in the Church's Teaching on Religious Life*, SCRIS, 1983.

FT *Faciem tuam, Domine, requiram* CICLSAL,[1] 2008

FLC	*Fraternal Life in Community*, CICLSAL, 1994.
PI	*Potissimum Institutioni*, CICLSAL, 1990.
RC	*Renovationis Causam,* SCRIS, 1969
RHP	*Religious and Human Promotion,* SCRIS, 1980

OTHERS

AFER	*African Ecclesial Review*
Ed./Eds	Editor/Editors
NIV	*New International Version*
OK	*Ordens Korrespondenz*
PL	*Patrologia Latina*
RB	*Regula Benedicti*

Notes

1. *CICLSAL* – Congregation for Institute of Consecrated Life and for Societies of Apostolic Life (formerly SCR and SCRIS). *SCR* – Sacred Congregation for Religious. *SCRIS* – Sacred Congregation for Religious and for Secular Institutes.

Dedicated to my parents
Mr Isaac Emeakaraoha Njoku
&
Mrs Cecilia Nwamaria Njoku
both of blessed memory.

In everlasting gratitude to them
for laying the foundation of my life as a Religious

PREFACE

My heart is filled with joy and gratitude as I undertake this work. It marks the silver jubilee of my monastic consecration as a member of the Benedictine 'Word Incarnate', Paschal Abbey, Nike Enugu Nigeria. It also coincides with the year for consecrated life. Both celebrations offer me the unique opportunity of a renewed reflection on the vocation to the Consecrated Life, to share its beauty and joy as well as its depth and mystery with the wider society.

Therefore, with a heart overflowing with thanksgiving and appreciation, I thank God, the Father Almighty through whom every good thing comes, for having sustained me in this journey until now and for having supported me in this research.

I desire to thank all those who have in one way or the other contributed to the successful completion of this book. In a especial way I thank Rev. Prof. Dr Pius Engelbert OSB, Rev. Fr Dr John Iwe, Rev. Fr Dr Anthony Igbekele and Sr Dr Makrina Finlay OSB, for critically proof-reading the draft of this work.

I also express my profound gratitude to Mother Abbess Franziska Lukas OSB, Sr Monica Lewis OSB and all the nuns of the Benedictine Abtei St Scholastika Dinklage Germany, for granting me a favourable environment that made this research work possible.

I also thank the members of my monastic family, Paschal Abbey, Nike Enugu and all the nuns of our filial houses; Nativity Monastery at Umuahia, Presentation Monastery at Idah and Visitation Monastery at Awka for their love and prayers that sustained me during this time.

In addition, I express my abiding thanks to Most Rev. Lucius Iwejuru Ugorji, DD, Bishop of Umuahia, for reading through the draft of this book and graciously endorsing it with an imprimatur.

Last but not the least, I wish to express my immense gratitude to my family who facilitated my initial consecration in baptism and promoted my vocation to the religious life in a healthy Christian environment.

I hope this work will not only be beneficial to priests and religious, seminarians and novices but also to the lay faithful who wish to grow in holiness.

Sr Mary Bride Njoku OSB

FOREWORD

In a world marked by 'a heightened individualism, a crisis of identity and a cooling of fervour,'[1] Rev. Sr Dr Mary Bride Njoku OSB, offers us in her masterpiece: *Consecrated Life: A Renewed Insight*, a profound vision of consecrated life.

Tracing it back to the religious identity of Christ she pointed out that the consecrated life is based on four basic, essential and inseparable elements: *Consecratio*, *Missio*, *Oratio* and *Communio*.

Through the religious *Consecratio* (consecration), she said, the religious express their strong desire to go the extra mile in 'being perfect'. This religious perfection, according to her, means continuously *striving for* and not *settling for*. It means 'spending one's life trying and struggling relentlessly to do God's will.' It is within this context that she developed a deep theology of the vows which she affirms, is 'both active and dynamic; a *process of becoming* poor, chaste and obedient and not a state that one arrives on the day of profession.'

Sr Mary Bride argues, quoting the Apostolic Exhortation of St John Paul II *Redemptionis Donum* that the real *Missio* (apostolate of the religious) is *what* and *who* they are to the ecclesial Church. It is not in the work they do but in the life they live; in their being an *eschatological presence* and being a *proleptic sign* of the Kingdom. This fact should manifest itself in whatever duty or assignment they undertake.

Referring to *Oratio* (prayer), she said is the hidden source of energy for their whole life. It constitutes 'living entirely in and out of a relationship with God, being open to His penetrating and transforming spirit and to the experience of both his presence and his absence'. It is the mystical aspect of the religious life.

Ultimately, Sr Mary Bride insists that *Communio* (community life) being an essential element of religious life is central and important to living the vows. The experience of unity in the interrelatedness of the members exposes them to unavoidable vulnerability before one another. This means that religious community life becomes a place of forgiveness *par excellence* because it is quite often burdened by conflict and so calls always for reconciliation.

As a good teacher and retreat preacher, Sr Mary Bride Njoku OSB, has really addressed the actual problems the religious communities face today. She has also offered some practical suggestions that could help to combat it. In fact, as someone who has been in the Formation House for some time, I find this work wonderful, very inspiring, enlightening, and educative. This is because it touches the fundamental, theological, liturgical, pastoral and psychological roots of religious life. I would, therefore, recommend it as a *Vademecum* (handbook) for all religious, both those who are aspiring to join the Religious Life and those who are already in it, and even for priestly formation.

Very Rev. Fr John Chijioke Iwe,
Rector Emeritus,
Seat of Wisdom Seminary, Owerri

1 Pope Francis, Apostolic Exhortation on the Proclamation of the Gospel in Today's World, *Evangelii Gaudium,* 78.

INTRODUCTION

> All his life long, wherever Jesus looked he saw the world not in terms simply of its brokenness - a patchwork of light and dark calling forth in us now our light, now our dark – but in terms of the ultimate mystery of God's presence buried in it like a treasure buried in a field ... To be whole, I believe, is to see the world like that. To see the world like that, as Jesus saw it, is to be whole. And sometimes I believe that even people like you and me see it like that. Sometimes even in the midst of our confused and broken relationships with ourselves, with each other, with God, we catch glimpses of that holiness and wholeness that is not ours by a long shot and yet is part of who we are.[1]

THIS WORK BEGINS with the assertion that there is a problem with the understanding of religious vocation today. It is an identity crisis which touches not just religious brothers or sisters, but also religious and diocesan priests. It is an identity crisis not just in the self-understanding of the religious themselves, but of an understanding of other Christian vocations of religious life in general. The questions asked are: What in the world are religious, for? Who are they? What do they stand for? What do they believe? How are they to order their lives? These questions invite us to re-examine their identity and to articulate the correct understanding of the nature and purpose of the religious life in the Church. Answers to such questions are in some way, what every book on religious life or theology seeks to answer. There is a general air of malaise, 'of identity crisis, involving disorientation and role confusion' which, 'is engulfing the world today.'[2]

There are two major reasons behind this religious crisis of identity.

The first reason is the continuous involvement of the laypeople in the service of the Church. In the Western world, the role of the laypeople in the service of the Church has proved to be a threat to the religious. This, however, has only revealed the fact that the religious themselves may not have fully appreciated their real identity. They believed that their *raison d'être* was the apostolate which they accomplish in the Church. But when they saw that most of those work they consider theirs are gradually being taken over by the laypeople they became confused and asked themselves, 'What then is the meaning of our lives as religious? What use are we to the ecclesial community?' This is a role-confusion that is shaking religious life to its foundation, so much so that they seem totally unidentifiable and *incognito*.

The second reason is the temptation to go always where the world takes them, to drift with whatever current happens to be the strongest. In other words, they are in constant danger of being, 'not actors in the drama of their own lives, but reactors'.[3] The fragmentary nature of their experience shatters them into fragments. Instead of being whole, as was the suggestion of St Paul in 1 Corinthians 7:34, most of the time they are in pieces, and they see the world in pieces, full of darkness at one moment and full of light at the next, distracted from their goal.

The world values achievements and purposefulness. In a word, it values '*doing*' over '*being*'. This has made it that many religious houses are now turned into 'career institutions' and no longer a place of becoming whole and holy. This is because religious themselves often judge themselves from the point of view of the world around them and no longer from a conviction based on Gospel values. It is because of this that Michael Casey said that they should be sceptical 'regarding secular ideologies of human fulfilment and the ability to follow a style of life which goes against the conventional wisdom propagated by the organs of popular culture'. The religious needs to learn to 'endure ridicule: whether we practise what we profess or not'.[4] Unless the religious learns to do this they will never come to terms with their true identity.

The Christian life is a journey towards wholeness; we are all in the *process* of becoming whole and holy. We all carry within us something of the holiness of our origin. Sinners are made in the image of God no less than saints, even a dead sparrow by the roadside is transparent to holiness. By taking the vows the religious announces publicly his/her intention to intensely embark in this *process* of becoming whole and holy. It is not an end point nor a static state of wholeness. The brother/sister who takes a vow of poverty, chastity and obedience does not become poor, chaste and obedient just by pronouncing those vows. Instead he/she vows *into the process* of becoming poor, chaste and obedient. So they have not yet arrived at their goal but have just announced to the public that they have started; and this journey which the religious has started on the day of his/her profession continues till death.

Therefore this work is geared towards precluding two things:

- Presumption or pretence on the part of any religious – as if they became poor, chaste and obedient on the day of their religious profession.
- Assumption or belief on the part of any Christian or the onlookers that the religious are poor, chaste and obedient from the day of their religious

profession. They (the religious) have their clay feet more or less like the rest of humanity. On the day of profession, however, they pledge themselves to *intensely* embark in this *process* of being whole and holy. This is a continuous struggle until death.

With this in mind, this work is going to examine these questions to see if it could at least understand the problem because to know what the problem is, is half the solution. The aim is not to supply answers to such questions but a contribution in analysing them.

This work starts therefore by attempting to classify the theological identity of religious life. When considering this, we will look at the vows and the culture of the lived lifestyle. But it seems that the best place to begin is to look at how Jesus himself lived, his religious identity and what he called his disciples to do. Those elements; *consecratio, missio, oratio,* and *communio* that formed Christ's religious identity which he transmitted by way of example to his disciples and were successively handed down to us shall be treated in the subsequent chapters two, three, four and five.

Therefore, starting with the religious consecration which is a dimension of primary importance, the work treats the theology of vows as a religious culture lifestyle. The living out of the religious consecration in practical terms is experienced in living the vows as a dynamic process of becoming poor, chaste and obedient. The necessary skills for entering into this dynamic process of the vows is assimilated during the preparatory or formative years. Furthermore, the 'workshop'[5] where the religious day by day lives out the fullness of this consecration is the community, fraternal life in common.

The last chapter will eventually demonstrate the fact that adherence to the person of Christ in prayer is the heart, the source, the sustenance and the condition for self-fulfillments as a religious. At the end, the work will reveal that the unity or the discord between *consecratio* and *missio* is a contributing factor in the identity crisis of religious life. In order to find out the real relationship between the two, the Church's documents will be used extensively.

Religious life is a journey of a lifelong *process* of becoming whole, holy and becoming what we are: the image and likeness of God. It is a joyous, spontaneous, self-forgetting and self-emptying response to what is most real: the world is holy because God made it so. Each one of us is called to holiness. When we lost this holiness due to sin, God sent His Son Jesus Christ, who was in *forma Dei,* but was not afraid to renounce his privileged status. He emptied and humbled himself (Philippians 2:6-7). He displaced himself willingly and lost his *forma,* his beauty and was disfigured to the point of being no longer recognizable (Isaiah 53:2) so as to bring us closer to God. He abolished the division that existed between us and God. This is the

One the religious is called to follow through same sort of displacement and emptying because the servant is not greater than the master. To deny this reality is to exist as a stranger in a world of strangers, disoriented and confused. To live out of and towards this reality is, little by little, to become whole, holy and religious.

Notes

1 Frederick BUECHNER, 'Journey Towards Wholeness', in: *Theology Today* 49, 1993, pp.454-464, here p. 454.

2 Bishop Lucius Iwejuru UGORJI, Sermon on the Golden Jubilee of a Priest, Port Harcourt 2013.

3 Expression borrowed from Frederick BUECHNER, 'Journey Towards Wholeness' p. 455.

4 Michael CASEY, 'Consecrated Chastity: Reflections on the Text of Gertrude of Helft', in: *Tjurunga* (*An Australasian Benedictine Review)* 31 1986, pp.3-14, here p.8.

5 'Workshop' here taken in the Benedictine sense of a group of people fraternally gathered together who are seriously engaged in a work or on a creative project. In RB 4:78, St Benedict speaks of a community as a workshop where all the virtues or what he called 'tools for good work' are faithfully carried out.

I

THEOLOGICAL IDENTITY OF RELIGIOUS LIFE

BEFORE GOING INTO the theme of our research it is necessary to have a quick excursus. A short historical survey would help to bring out the link that exists between the New Testament and the religious life. This would in turn help to throw light on the value and proper identity of the religious life in the Church. This sketchy historical overview should be read as a history of the working of the Holy Spirit who animated men and women to model their lives on that of Jesus and on that of the Apostles.

1. *Short Historical Excursus*

There are three different stages in the history of religious life: the patristic times, the medieval times to the period of Reformation and Renaissance and lastly Vatican II till today.

1. The first stage, the *patristic period*, which is also the era of the birth of the Christian monasticism (hence both go hand in hand), had laid emphasis on the *obedient listening* of the believer to the *Word of God*. An exemplary figure of this trend was St Anthony of Egypt (c. 251-356), whose life was written by St Athanasius. The ideal way for such listening was withdrawal into the desert in order to live out the Gospel: a quest for God alone and a thirst for prayer. As master of the eremitical life, St Anthony sold everything he had and gave the proceeds to the poor (cf. Matthew 19:21). Gradually as other hermits sought out spiritual guides an evolution began to take place towards the coenobitic form of life. Of significant influence in this process was Pachomius (292–346), who was known as the father of coenobitism. With the careful reading of the Word of God, he gave existence to life in communion with the brothers (cf. Acts 2:44). After Pachomius came Basil the Great (330–379) who underlined the experience of the primitive community and gave much value to meditation on the Word of God. He gathered around him a group of like-minded disciples, stressing the aspect of fraternity among all the believers; men and women, monks and laity alike seen as the living Body of Christ (cf. Acts 4:32-35). At this first stage in the life of the Church,

the Gospels and other biblical texts were used as base for the foundation of the religious life. Such texts are: Acts 2:42-47, 4:32-35; the Sermon on the Mount especially the Beatitudes (Matthew 5-7); the passage on Mary and Martha of Bethany (cf. Luke 10:38-42) was used as a justification for the existence of the active and contemplative lives in the Church. In this prospect some fathers like Cassian (c. 360–435)[1] saw the Church as originally monastic in character based on the model of the apostolic community founded by Jesus. This is not far from the truth because there are in the history of the patristic period an abundant evidence for such supposition.

2. The *medieval period* took over and developed this theological vision of religious life as witnessed in the lives of different monks, hermits, canon Regulars, Mendicants, not only men but also women. J.-M.R. Tillard has summarized[2] the two movements of that period as that of the *integral Christian life,* a conceptual framework for Christian living that goes back to Eusebius, Jerome and Cassian. The second movement which distinguished between *precepts* and *counsels* has its origins in Origen of Alexandria, flowered in the Scholastic epoch and has survived till Vatican II. It sees the religious life as a state of perfection. The existence of two different concepts of being a Christian has been stressed and well articulated in the Church, especially from the 12th century. There are two ways

of being a Christian: one of the ways which is seen to be common to all Christians is the observance of the *evangelical precepts* and the second way is believed to be reserved for those who wish to live according to the *evangelical counsels* (Matthew 19:10-12; 16-30; 1 Corinthians 7:25-35; Acts 2:42-44; 4:32). The first way was reserved for laypeople, while the second way which aims at the state of evangelical perfection was reserved for priests and religious. The classical texts for such a dualistic conception of being a Christian was taken from the evangelical episode of the rich young man in Matthew 19:16-22, where Jesus himself said to the rich young man 'If you want to be perfect, go, sell what you possess… come, follow me.' (v.21). Meanwhile there have been many proponents of these dualistic understanding of being Christians starting from the Middle Ages till today.[3] So taking its justification from the word of Jesus, the religious express publicly their wish to follow Christ by means of the religious vows of Poverty, Chastity and Obedience.

3. A big change came with the *Second Vatican Council* and its demands for a return to the sources of the Gospel (PC 2), and its stress on the universal call to holiness (LG 40), coupled with the fruitful studies of modern exegetes and the theological debate on the relationship between *baptismal and religious consecration*. All these were meant to re-establish the

relationship between the Christian life and religious life and in the light of this, religious life was no longer seen as a state of perfection but as a radical way of living the common Christian vocation.[4] Religious life according to the Council is positioned in the heart of the Church as a determining element in as much as 'it expresses the intimate nature of the Christian vocation'[5] and a divine gift to the Church and becomes the living icon of the relationship between Christ and the Church because 'it imitates more closely and perennially represents in the Church the form of life lived by the Son of God when he was on earth doing the will of the Father.'[6]

2. *Christological Dimension of Religious Life: Vatican II*

In the light of the Vatican II *magisterium*, the central element of the theological identity of the religious life has been and still is the Christological element, which however is the most valid and fruitful dimension of the theology of religious life. This Christological character is expressed in two different ways: the first refers to the biblical figure of Christ. Thus, religious life is seen as the continuation of the life of Christ; the second refers to the figure of the disciples or the apostles of Christ: religious life is the continuation of the following of Christ proposed by Him to his disciples, of which the apostles were the principal proponents. In the dogmatic Constitution *Lumen*

Gentium, the figure of the religious is so profoundly related to the figure of Jesus. The evangelical counsels must not be presented as abstract realities, but as concrete and essential features of a chaste, poor and obedient Jesus. Therefore, we are not living the life of the vows primarily because we want to do what Jesus said, but rather because we want to live as he lived, that is why the religious life is sometimes called 'imitation of Christ'. The document says that 'the religious state constitutes a closer imitation and an abiding re-enactment in the Church of the form of life which the Son of God made his own when he came into the world to do the will of the Father and which he propounded to the disciples who followed him' (LG 44).

According to the Second Vatican Council's Decree on the up-to-date Renewal of Religious Life, *Perfectae Caritatis,* to renew religious life is above all to bring it as close as possible to its source: the Christ of the Gospel. Taken in this way, therefore, the following of Christ proposed in the Gospel must be considered by all Institutes as the supreme rule for an authentic renewal. Thus the document says: 'Since the final norm of the religious life is the following of Christ as it is put before us in the Gospel, this must be taken by all institutes as the supreme rule'(PC 2a). This means that to investigate on the evangelical foundation of the consecrated life, the best track to follow is to have a look at the person of Jesus, to the structure of his religious existence. Thus PC 1 again says that the pursuit of perfect charity by means of the evangelical counsels traces its origins to the teaching and the example of the Divine Master. To this effect, Saint John Paul II's 1996 Apostolic Exhortation *Vita Consecrata,* which has become the '*Magna Carta*' for an effective renewal of religious life, says: 'The evangelical basis of consecrated life is to be sought in the special relationship which Jesus, in his earthly life, established with some of his disciples. He called them not only to welcome the Kingdom of God into their own lives, but also to put their lives at its service, leaving everything behind and closely imitating his own *way of life*' (VC 14).

3. Jesus' Religious Identity

The passage of the Scripture where Christ defined his religious identity is that pronounced in the synagogue, where he applied to himself the text of Isaiah 61:1-2, 'The spirit of the Lord has been given to me, for he has anointed me. He has sent me to bring good news to the poor, to proclaim liberty to captives and to the blind new sight, to set the downtrodden free, to proclaim the Lord's year of favour to the poor' (Luke 4:16-18). Here Jesus underlined two important elements that are strictly related to one another: *consecration* and *mission*: the consecration by the Holy Spirit in union with the Father (John 10:30; 14:11) and the mission he received from the Father and lived in obedience to the will of the Father (John 4:34; 10:36; 20:21; Hebrews 3:1). Jesus lived his life of consecration by totally belonging to the Father and this gave meaning to the total donation of himself to the service of the brothers. The consecration of Christ both on the active and passive sense, and the type of mission or apostolate that he engaged in are clearly depicted in the following Scripture passages:

- John 10:36: '…someone the Father has consecrated and sent into the world.'
- Acts 10:38: 'God had anointed him with the Holy Spirit and with power, and because God was with him, Jesus went about doing good and curing all who had fallen into the power of the devil.'
- John 17:18-19: 'As you sent me into the world, I have sent them into the world, and for their sake I consecrate myself so that they too may be consecrated in truth.'
- Luke 4:16-18: 'He has sent me to bring good news to the poor, to proclaim liberty to captives and to the blind new sight, to set the downtrodden free, to proclaim the Lord's year of favour to the poor.'
- Luke 7:22: '…the blind see again, the lame walk, lepers are cleansed, and the deaf hear, the dead are raised to life, the Good News is proclaimed to the poor and happy is the man who does not lose faith in me.'
- Matthew 9:36-37: 'And when he saw the crowds, he

> had *compassion* on them, because they were harassed and helpless, like sheep without a shepherd. Then he said to his disciples: "The harvest is rich but the labourers are few, so ask the Lord of the harvest to send out labourers to his harvest."'

We can see from the above texts that the religious experience lived by Jesus was marked by his consecration to the Father and by his mission towards men, (*consecration* and *mission*) then the energy which sustains him was drawn from above Luke 5:16 (prayer). Like Christ every religious is consecrated by the Father in the Holy Spirit – a deepening of the consecration already received in baptism. The passive aspect of consecration is a priority in the consecration of Christ, who is the supreme consecrated One in human history. Thus he says; 'For them I consecrate myself' (John 17:19). With an impressive summary St John Paul II describes the harmony of the elements of Christ's consecration: 'Accepting his consecration by the Father, the Son in turn consecrates himself to the Father' (VC 22a). We cannot really and truly say that we have consecrated ourselves to God in the same way as Christ, for He is the only One who can truly say that, because consecration is a special grace received from God. The passive role which we played is as a consequence of us being human beings endowed with freedom and responsibility before the sanctifying action of God.

A close observation of the above Scriptural passages highlights to us Christ's active and passive consecration, pinpointing to us the subject of his mission: the poor, infirm, less-privileged, those who do not know their need of God, in a word, all the 'sinned-againsts' of the society. His apostolate is love, concern and care for the less privileged of the society. Therefore, 'Religious consecration manifests in a concrete and eloquent way a *preferential love for Christ* – for Christ present in the Holy Eucharist, for Christ as he lives today in the poor and the sick, in the elderly and in children, in families and in persons from broken homes. By the same token, a preferential love for Christ means a preference for what Christ loves, a desire to have the same attitude as Christ himself (cf. Philippians 2:5ff), a longing to see God's 'kingdom come on earth as it is in heaven.'[7]

Furthermore, Christ, who was always in communion with the Father in the Holy Spirit, called his Apostles to be with him so that later He would send them out on mission (cf. Mark 3:14). As He sent them out, he promised He would be with them every day till the end of the ages (cf. Matthew 28:20). Thus Christ's earthly life is based on four pillars: *Consecratio*, *Missio*, *Oratio* and *Communio*. Then the Apostles, whom he called to Himself, continued His way of life (Act 2:42-47). So it is that the religious life is founded on these four pillars.

4. *The Four Pillars of Religious Life*

Religious life is built on the four pillars of *consecratio, missio, oratio* and *communio.* Although distinct from one another, these pillars are interdependent and if any one of them is removed, the result is something other than religious life. Thus any theology of religious life is either implicitly or explicitly based on the combination of and interaction between all four of these elements. The chart below offers an overview:[8]

***Consecratio* – Consecration**	***Missio* – Mission/ Apostolate**	***Oratio* – Prayer/ Liturgical & Personal**	***Communio* – Community**
Life from God	Love: Living for others	Life for God	Living in a community
Facing the Father	Facing the people especially the less privileged, the sinned-against and sinners	Praising God	Face-to-face encounter with one another
Encountering God	Being there for others and encountering the suffering humanity	Being there for God: bringing the pains and the suffering humanity to Him	Shaping & being shaped by the community
Total dedication of oneself	Selfless Service: love in action	Contemplation and praise	Relationship; with physical presence which challenges us, with their pain & their pleas, with all its anguish, turmoil and all its graces, which affects us in our close & continuous interaction

Consecratio **– Consecration**	***Missio*** **– Mission/ Apostolate**	***Oratio*** **– Prayer/ Liturgical & Personal**	***Communio*** **– Community**
Vertical: To heaven	To the earth and its realities	Meeting point for heaven and earth	Horizontal: At eye level with our fellow brothers/sisters
I	All	The Church as the Body of Christ	We
From the Father	With and through Christ	Doxology	In the Spirit

A closer look at these four elements, makes clear that *Consecratio*, *Missio* and *Communio* are united in what can be called 'an equilateral triangle' and that *Oratio* serves as the heart that stands in the middle of the other three and is the life source for any religious vocation. A question which is worth posing is whether one should recognize the three elements as having equal rank, or whether *Consecratio* should be singled out as the source out of which *Missio* and *Communio* flow. Regardless of how that question is answered, the place of *oratio* in the life of a religious must certainly be treated separately. It is the quiet centre, the heartbeat which supports and sustains religious life; often unnoticeably, unless, of course, it stops beating. This mystical aspect of the religious life is indispensable: it constitutes living entirely in and out of a relationship with God, being open to his penetrating and transforming spirit and to the experience of both his presence and his absence while all the while seeking his nearness and living by his grace. It also leads us to witnessing to him through the acceptance of suffering, and by living in and communicating him to others. These four elements are part and parcel of the religious way of life.

We have seen so far that in the course of history, the patristics laid emphasis on the *obedient listening to the word of God* and the medievals gave different interpretations on the following of Christ by means of *evangelical precepts* and *evangelical counsels.* The Vatican II in *Lumen Gentium* brought back the image of Christ at the centre of religious quest because the religious is not so much there to do what Christ said as to live as He lived. Religious life from then on has become a living like, with and for Christ. This implies not only an interior adherence to the person of Christ but, equally, a total commitment to him. The religious vocation consequently becomes a matter of continuing the same project of salvation as Jesus did in human history. One does this by taking on the attitudes and the behaviours which were characteristic of him, which in some way, are summed up in terms of poverty, chastity and obedience. The initiation into these attitudes and behaviours are done by means of religious consecration.

Notes

1 See Jean CASSIEN, Conférences : in : *Sources Chrétiennes* 64, Ed. Par. E. PICHERY, Paris 1959, III, pp. 14-16; A. DEVOGNE, ‹ Monachisme et Eglise dans la pensée de Cassien ’, in :Id., *Téologie de la vie monastique. Etudes sur la tradition patristique*, Cerf, Paris 1961, pp. 213-240.

2 See the studies of J.-M.R. TILLARD; Davanti a Dio e per il mondo. Il progetto dei religiosi, Paoline, Alba 1975, pp. 108-133; Id., 'Consigli evangelici', in: *Dizionario degli Istituti di Perfezione*, II Paoline, Roma 1975, pp. 1630-1685.

3 See the Studies of J.-M.R. TILLARD; 'Davanti a Dio e per il mondo', pp. 108-133.

4 See S. TASSOTTI, La consacrazione religiosa. Dal Concilio Vaticano II all'Esortazione Apostolica *'Vita Consecrata',* OCD, Città di Castello 2003.

5 Vatican Council II, Decreto sull'attività Missionaria della Chiesa *Ad Gentes*, 18.

6 Vatican II Cost. Dogmatica sulla Chiesa *Lumen Gentium*, 44; see also Paul VI, Esortazione *Apostolica: Evangelii nuntiandi* (8 Decembre 1975), 69.

7 John Paul II, 'Il Religioso testimonia al mondo una vita dedicate tutta a Dio' (10-11 Marzo 1986) in: *INFORMATIONES S.C.R.I.S. (Sacra Congregazione per i Religiosi e gli Istituti Secolari),* XII, n. 1 1986, p.75.

8 The idea for the chart below is taken from Stefan Kiechle, with huge modification and personal touch. See Stefan KIECHLE, *Consecratio – Communio – Missio*. Die drei Grundelemente des Ordenslebens, in: Margareta GRUBER, Stefan KIECHLE (eds.), *Gottes Freundschaft. Ordensleben heute denken*, Echter Verlag GmbH, Würzburg, 2007, pp. 51-71, here p. 51. The positions for these four elements is based on the way they were presented in the Scriptures, i.e., *Consecratio, missio, oratio* and *communion.* With the Apostles we have a strong community base in Acts 2.

II

CONSECRATION

FOR THE PAST CENTURIES, religious life was most comprehensively thought of as a life of the vows. These vows are usually identified in the triad of poverty, chastity and obedience. But the Church, in Vatican II and in all subsequent official documents, has moved away from this emphasis on the vows in order to stress the notion of '*Consecratio*' as the true foundation of religious life. By stressing *Consecratio*, Vatican II has challenged religious to live out their particular call from God, that initial call of the Divine Master who says: 'Come and See', and to live out their vocational responsibility to be, above all else, women and men who consciously strive to imitate Jesus and his values in their thoughts, words and deeds. The negative reaction of some religious to the Church's use of the word *Consecratio* as central to religious life likely arises from an almost instinctive fear of this awesome responsibility and a desire to escape from it. Sometimes, too, there is a negative response to the use of 'consecration' because the word is so identified with a 'setting apart for sacred use'.

From the theological point of view, consecration involves three parties: God himself who calls and consecrates; the individual who responds to God's call and the Church which accepts the candidate as a member of the religious community. These two latter parties are the ones that can be seen but, of necessity, they are secondary. These latter two give a response to consecration for in reality, consecration is the action of God and consequently, only God consecrates, because God, the Holy One, alone makes holy. So the basis of consecration is God's initiative in calling people to Himself, just as the initiative of baptism is the Lord's call. Religious life is a deeper entry into the same consecration as baptism because the religious is responding to a further call of God to enter into the baptismal life and life-patterns of Jesus.[1]

However, vowed consecration may not only mean that someone has been 'set apart', at least not in the sense that this phrase is often used. This is because Jesus came to proclaim the holiness of all creation. Holiness therefore, is the task of every human being and indeed, of everything that exists. It is the universal call to give glory to God by being who and what we are. The world is the break-through of God for He said 'I have conquered the world' (John 16:33) and so the world is sacred, therefore, no one needs to be 'set apart from it'. Sandra Schneider insists that by means of the Incarnation which is, in its essence, God's embodiment, God becomes part of His creation.[2] God in Jesus shows us that there is no divide between heaven and earth, no need for a bridge. Human things become divinized and divine things become humanized. Human beings therefore do not need to be set apart from the world and made superior to it in order to mediate between heaven and earth.

1. Religious Consecration demands 'Extra Quality' and not 'Setting Apart'

Religious life in its essence is a life about 'a more', an 'extra', doing something more, offering something more, giving one's life more to God, going deeper into one's baptismal promises. One who felt called expresses the desire of wanting to go an extra mile to be more like Christ, to be closer to Christ, to be of greater service to Christ and his Church. Jesus said: 'If you want to be perfect, go, sell what you possess … come, follow me' (Matthew 19:21-24). There cannot be a religious life without the quality of going an extra mile. This quality of going an extra mile revolves around an exclusive love-relationship with Christ, an embracing of his values and a desire to spend one's life in bringing about the Kingdom. It would be an anomaly for anyone to enter into religious life with the intention of doing the bare minimum since the very essence of the life is situated only in the 'more'. What we often describe as the 'radicalism' in the following of Jesus in religious life is caught in the expression of 'more', or 'extra mile'. This 'more' is the locus of the initiating call of God, and the vows, however numbered and named, spell out this 'more'. This 'more' quality is what Christ meant when he said to the rich young man: 'If you wish to be perfect, go sell all and come follow me.'

By virtue of our religious consecration we are required to counteract the human tendency of becoming settled in such a way that allows us to forget the fundamentally unsettled position that we share with all people. Voluntary displacement as a response to God's call leads us unswervingly to the recognition of our inner brokenness. Voluntary displacement is thus central to our lives as religious. In it we experience our true condition, which is, that like everyone else we are pilgrims on the way, sinners in need of grace. That is why for us religious, 'consecration' does not mean that someone has been 'set apart' in an unlimited way. Since in this displacement we experience that we are sinners like our brothers and sisters it also follows that we are not to be set apart from them. When God became human, he entered into solidarity with us. He became our equal and our intimate not just to bridge but to abolish the distance that we perceive between God and humanity. If we are vowing the evangelical counsel, then we are vowing to living according to the Gospels. Consecration in the community of the New Testament involves neither separation nor superiority. Through his work of unification between God and humanity, Jesus has given us a radically new understanding of consecration. To be consecrated is to be holy; to be united with God in the love poured forth in our hearts by the Holy Spirit (cf. Romans 5:5). It is to live in the reality that the fullness of Divine love enlightens the darkness and sets the earth on fire with the very flame that Jesus came to enkindle. We have been sent into the world as Jesus was sent into the world to bring salvation by *solidarity with* not by *separation from* those to whom we are sent.[3]

In this case, to take vows or rather to be consecrated does not mean to be made more sacred, because we are already sacred and the world in which we are in is also sacred. In Genesis we read that God saw that creation was good and celebrated that goodness. Even when taking into account the fall of humanity and the entry of sin into the world, it remains certain that the world cannot be something different from what God declared all creation to be. This might be uncomfortable for some of us and might lead us to a crisis of identity. After all, if we are not 'set apart' what are we?

In What Sense is the Consecrated Life a 'Setting Apart'

Consecration is from Latin *cum* 'with' and *sacrare* to

'make sacred'. In the strict sense it means: 'the total dedication of a person or a thing to God and his service, and its subsequent separation from ordinary human use. What is consecrated thereafter belongs exclusively to God.'[4] In baptism we were all consecrated and are therefore set apart for God and His service. Religious consecration being a deepening of the baptismal consecration is not meant to make the religious more sacred than they are by baptism nor is it supposed to set them apart from those who are already set apart, that is to say, it does not in any way mean 'a double setting apart'. Instead religious consecration is an intensification of the initial baptismal setting apart from the 'world'.[5]

Religious are therefore expected to *fervently* and *zealously* transcend the values of this world, by distancing themselves from the *ways of the world*. This has nothing to do with *fuga mundi,* but a simple being in the world, physically present, but not of the world, not part of its values (John 17:14-15). They are neither to engage in the sinful activities the world promotes nor retain the insipid, corrupt mind that the world creates. Rather, they are to conform themselves and their minds, to that of Christ Jesus (Romans 12:1-2). Instead of *thinking* and *acting* like the 'world', they are detached from this more common way of viewing and living life and are given a different purpose which is to model their lives on that of Christ who came to save the 'world'.[6] They ought therefore to be strangers to this world's system and are set apart from worldliness and mundane standards. It is in this intensification, this going of an extra mile, symbolized by the religious consecration, that Christ addressing the rich young man called 'being perfect'.

Religious Consecration: A Life of Perfection?

Where does the 'extra quality' of such a life of consecration reside? Perhaps it is in the general designation of religious life as a life of perfection. Can we, with confidence say that religious life is a life of perfection? Personally, I find this expression problematic because quite often it seems to be a life of imperfection. Experience has shown us that religious life is a place where all our imperfections are made visible. However, such an audacious presumption is based on Scriptural passages such as: 'If you want to be perfect, go, sell what you possess … come, follow me' (Matthew 19:21-24). 'You, therefore, must be perfect, as your heavenly Father is perfect' (Matthew 5:48).

What did Jesus have in mind when he spoke about perfection? When we use the word 'perfect' we are often talking about attaining a level that cannot be surpassed, about reaching a standard of excellence that cannot be improved. That is not, however, what Jesus had in mind. In his teaching, to be perfect is to become what God knows we can be. Jesus' call to perfection is meant to push us beyond the comfort zone of mediocrity towards excellence. It is meant to make us *strive* for, not *settle* for! Taken as a ground for the religious life, then we can say it is telling us to seek for something 'extra', to go for the 'more' quality of life, to deepen our baptismal consecration.

When the Lord summarizes his teaching about love with the call for perfection, he is insisting that we should not be satisfied with the mediocrity of loving those who love us and hating those who hate us. Loving the lovable and loathing the loathsome is not *striving for*, it's *settling for!* As Louis Lotz so poignantly expresses it: Jesus is asking us to seek 'that mature love which enables us to love the enemy and pray for the persecutor. He (is) saying that we should use all the potential for loving that we have within us, that we should hold nothing back. He (is) saying that we should be perfect!'[7]

In *The Thorn Birds* a 1977 novel by Colleen McCullough which, in 1983 was adapted into a television mini-series, the story is told of Ralph de Bricassart (Richard Chamberlain), a priest who was engaged in a constant struggle between his calling and his carnal desires. In the story he becomes a cardinal who works in the Vatican. The boy Dane admires him and wants to be just like him. Watching the film one is deeply touched by the encounter between this Fr Ralph and Dane. Here is the dialogue between the two:

Dane: Father, did you ever have any regret about entering the priesthood?

Ralph: Yes, inevitably I suppose. I missed things; a woman to share my life, perhaps even a son like you, I would have liked that very much.

Dane: What caused you then to make your decision to become a priest?

Ralph: Curiously, it was like an unconscious decision.

Dane: More like something that you've always known from the first?

Ralph: My fate you might say!

Dane: Father, I also want to be a priest.

Ralph: Why? You could do anything with your life, be anything!

Dane: How can you say that Father, when you are everything I would want to be.

Ralph: No, you know nothing of the man I am. You look at me and see the Cardinal, the prince of the Church.

Dane: No! I see the priest, *the perfect priest.*

Ralph: Then you are wrong. To say it was my fate to be a priest is not to say it was given to me like a gift. *An entire life time of trying to offer myself up totally to God* has brought me no more than moments of oneness with him and I have broken every vow. Do you understand? Every vow! I have not been equal to the sacrifice God asks.

Dane: But Father, *you have spent your life trying.*

> *Father, when I say the perfect priest, I didn't mean some infallible being. I mean someone who tries to do God's will. May be I wouldn't be equal to the sacrifice either. But if I don't try, my life will have no meaning. It is the only way I know to show God how much I love him, just by trying.*[8]

This is, for me, an outstanding description of what a 'life of perfection' really is. A life, as Dane puts it: 'spent *trying* to do God's will'. A religious should show God that he/she loves him by trying sincerely and continuously. This trying inevitably means falling and getting up and at each stage being aware of one's imperfection and starting over again and again. And this should not be surprising to us if we look at the apostles as described in the Bible or talk to anyone experienced in the religious life. A saying from the *Apophthegmata Patrum*[9] has it that when an old monk was asked what people do in the monastery, his reply was, 'Oh well, we fall and get up, we fall and get up, we fall and get up'. This is what a life of perfection means: trying, falling and getting up, and in so doing, coming ever closer to the Kingdom. Perhaps not with elegance but certainly with the help of God's grace. This inelegant struggle to put into practice the lofty goals of perfect love and union and this reliance on God's grace is the very essence of the 'more' quality; not settling, not staying down after falling, but getting back up.

Perfection is not a completed state of being; it is not an abstraction. It is the person of Jesus whom we grow towards and follow after in order to complete or mature ourselves. His perfection is complete; our perfection is in process. It is in this process by which we develop our discipleship; it is the 'following after' which the rich young man found so difficult. We 'follow towards' perfection even as Jesus, by his suffering and dying, by his living and rising, was perfected.[10]

The Enigma of the 'Life of Perfection'

When in entering the religious life, one embraces a life of supposed perfection, the inevitable but always surprising and discomforting result is that the person recognizes his or her own imperfections. There are two reasons for this:

a) Christ is the ideal model of the religious, therefore both conscious and unconscious confrontation of oneself with the ideal model certainly exposes the great difference. That is why holy people are in fact never aware of their holiness because what is always evident before their eyes is what is still lacking in them in order to conform their lives to that of Christ.

b) The second reason is that the more honest we are with ourselves, the clearer it is that we do not always seek that hard to imitate the life of Christ. We have not sought enough to say to our world that we are the manifestation of Christ. We have not been sincerely trying to do God's will. We are not indeed 'striving for' but we tend to 'settle for'.

A typical example is of Jacinta, a novice who went to her novice mistress asking for permission to leave the convent. When the novice mistress asked for a reason, she explained: 'Because, since I joined this Order my imperfections have increased in number. When I was in the parish I was looked up to, by everyone as a little angel. I used to be humble, silent, prayerful and I used to do dry fasting three times a week. But since I joined your Order, community life has brought out the worst in me. I can no longer bear it, I must leave'.

Of course, this novice is right in her assessment of herself, even if not of the situation at large. Religious life is, after all, a life where all our imperfections come to the fore thanks to a growing sensitivity to faults on our own part and also to community life which makes us so vividly aware of our shortcomings. However, our attitude towards these imperfections should not be to quit but to continuously fight against these imperfections, and to recognize that our very awareness of such faults is a chance to improve upon them. Certainly the Novitiate is a time to test a vocation and there are occasions when the novice experiences a sense of alienation, that is of not belonging and feels a deep emptiness and sometimes a sort of frustration, like in the case of Jacinta. It is a time of death and resurrection in which a novice is confronted with the significance of all his/her previous experiences, of all through which he/she has become the person he/she is now; 'an imperfect being', of all those whom he/she has left and whom he/she continues to love like family, friends and so on. So, as we grow in the religious life, we inevitably face situations like that of Jacinta in which we, together with others, must learn how to discern between those struggles which we should avoid completely because they could cause harm to our soul, and those which are difficult for us just because they stretch us and hurt our pride and selfish will.

With the constant manifestations of our imperfections, we can testify that the 'more' quality attached to the religious life is not meant as a claim of superiority for our own form of witness. We can become arrogant when we feel that God is asking more of us; we can court the idea that we are better than others for being able to make more sacrifices. In such cases, it is right to question whether the 'call' was really from God and to what extent selfish pride has taken over. Fortunately for us, the reality of our shortcomings often keeps our pride in check. But whether that is the case or not, by keeping Jesus' self-giving manner of life as our model, we must come more and more to the understanding that our goal in the religious life is not just to be better and holier than those around us but to manifest Jesus to a prodigal world. When we do this authentically, we cannot be selfish or proud and there is no choice but to take up our cross daily to follow him.

Perfection is that for which we make application of the Gospel and it is in perfection that the 'more' quality of religious life is spelled out. Even though we will not become perfect in this life, religious life appeals for the aim, for the desire, for the hope, for the strategy, for the application and for the labour. Labour towards perfection is never in vain. Every single moment spent in application towards becoming more and more like our Lord is time well spent. Perfection has to do with *being* as well as *doing*. It has to do with the moulding of character, of doing the things of Christ such that they and HE becomes our pattern. This is the aim of religious life; the imitation of our Lord. The aim and the desire of a religious should be to have the audacity to say to the world, 'I am seeking to imitate the very life that Christ lived while upon this earth.' Every opportunity for doing some good affords us an opportunity of being genuinely Christ-like. The trait of genuineness, an indispensable trait of his character, must also become part of our character. We must be honest with God, with ourselves, with our world, and with the Word of God. We must be honest! We must be genuine in what we are seeking to do in the name of Christ and for his Church. In religious life this 'honesty' tends to go by another name: humility.

2. Consecrated Celibacy and Consecrated Marriage

Religious vows in truth can be compared to matrimonial vows. Both of them give a particular shape to our baptismal consecration. The religious consecration is a continuation, a deepening and an attempt to give a concrete definition to our baptismal consecration. Christologically, it could be said that through his/her consecration, the religious is immersed into Christ's own consecration so that she/he could also pass through his cross unto his resurrection. To stress and bring out clearly the consistency between the religious/matrimonial consecration with the baptismal consecration some religious sisters/brothers in Germany who are still having with them their baptismal candles use the same candle on the day of their religious final consecration, as a strong symbolic sign of connection and cohesion. Those who are preparing for matrimonial consecration use theirs too. On 2 April 2014, Pope Francis concluding his series of catechesis dedicated to the sacraments said that 'Marriage responds to a specific vocation and must be considered as a consecration. The man and woman consecrate themselves in their love. Married couples, thanks to the Sacrament, are invested with a genuine mission, that of making visible, starting with simple and ordinary things, the love Christ has for His Church.'[11]

Through our choice to live celibately in a given community (Chastity), dispossessing ourselves of everything, sharing and having everything in common (Poverty) and listening to one another (Obedience), by doing all these, we bring our baptismal consecration to maturity. The primacy is on baptismal consecration and when we do this, we do it in *a different* and not in *a superior* way to others who choose to work out their consecration in other ways. Religious and other Christians are equally called to witness to the infinite love of God, but the richness of the mystery requires a variety of expressions. So, the witness, which the Christians are called to give, is not distinguished by locations on a scale of comparative excellence but by the aspect of the mystery of Divine Love that comes to special expression in various lives.

As between celibacy and married life there is no moral superiority of the one state over the other. Though the knowledge that a person is devoted to celibacy for some good motive will always tend to command respect, because we are all aware that it is not an easy choice but on the whole then it may be concluded that there is no good ground for pressing the doctrine of the counsels as indicating short-cuts to perfection. I believe that there are no short-cuts to perfection, for every vocation has got its hard ways and somehow mild ways. What is certain is that all are intended for perfection, and that all may make progress towards perfection however they may be situated and the advice is: Let each man, wherein he was called, therein abide with God.

The witness of each Christian vocation, says Schneider, is rich but limited and therefore an adequate witness to the mystery of Divine love can only be given in mutuality and complementarities with other Christians. There are therefore diverse ways in which we give response to the Creator's break-through and religious life is one way in which we do that. The Divine love experienced in all its richness by each, is too multifaceted to be manifested by any one life. In this way, consecrated celibacy, i.e. religious life, consecrated marriage, i.e. the sacrament of matrimony and what today is called the 'single lay life' are mutually necessary vocations which together witness to the central mystery revealed in the incarnation in the never-ending redemptive intimacy of God with us. Everyone is called to experience the fullness of this mystery, but each is called to witness to it in the limited way possible by one's own gifts incarnated into one of the many life styles open to us. The humility by which we realize both our limitations and our giftedness opens us to an appreciation of the mutuality of witnesses in the Church. There is a danger that communities of Religious brothers and sisters fall for a temptation to set themselves up as 'something special'. It is good in any calling to be proud of it and to think that other people do not know what they are missing. But the truth is that each one is as good as the other.

The 'Extra Quality' Expressed in the Evangelical Counsels

Religious life, as a particular form of *sequela Christi* (following of Christ), has its concrete expression in the radicalization of poverty, chastity and obedience with the desire to imitate Christ, poor, chaste, and obedient, and of living like him in view of the Kingdom. Called to follow and radically imitate Christ, the religious should strive for a greater uniformity of life in Christ. The radical following of Jesus, poor, chaste and obedient, brings into play especially the practice of the three evangelical counsels, which is an attempt to concretely live out this quality of going an extra mile. Though the evangelical counsels do not exhaust the essence and the demands of such a life of consecration, they are signs that whoever freely and willingly accepts the call is automatically opting for an additional and total surrender to the Gospel demands. For in this *sequela Christi*, it is a question of knowing him, of teaching about him and of living him through the radical living out of poverty, chastity and obedience. This 'radicality' in the following of the poor, chaste and obedient Christ is another word for 'extra quality of life'.

The Vows as a Process and a Culture Lifestyle

Just as in every art there is practice so also in the art of religious living there is practice and progressive steps towards what could be termed as 'the fullness'. A religious brother/sister both inwardly and outwardly goes through or learns a refined art of living in order to get into this religious-culture lifestyle, which the vows classify. St Benedict in his rule brought out clearly the dynamic element of the religious profession, which remains a *process* and not the end point of a *process* (like an end point of religious formation) and that is the very reason why the *Vita Consecrata* stresses the necessity for an ongoing formation after religious profession. The dynamic element of religious life can be summed up in one word '*conversio*' (conversion) and it is this *conversio* that we promised in our baptismal promises. The word *conversio* also recaps the triad: poverty, chastity and obedience. A converted person is automatically poor, chaste and obedient. That is why the Benedictines do not promise Poverty and Chastity because they are believed to be summed up under the word *conversio*. In the religious vows the process of this conversion is spelled out to the brother/sister. Thus, St Benedict spoke of the *beginning* of conversion '*initium conversationis*' (RB 73.1), *progress* in true conversion '*processu vero conversationis*' (Prologue 49) and *perfection* of conversion '*perfectionem conversationis*' (RB 73.2).[12] It is in this dynamic sense that conversion takes a semantic meaning of a continuous amendment of one's life and develops into a *process* of becoming, showing that it takes a lifetime to make a religious but in the meantime 'a depraved beast is going through a process of daily conversion through engagement with the grace of God.'[13] So being a religious is not what has happened to me on the day I pronounce my vows but it is what is continually happening to me. I try every day to become chaste, to be poor and to be obedient, if I happen to fail in any, I get up and move on until death and that is the character of it being a permanent way of life. The following poem from Andreas Knapp brings out the reality of this fact.

Gelübde	**Vow**
nein	No,
ich habe mich nicht versprochen	It was not a slip of the tongue
denn mein Versprechen gilt	So my promise is valid
in ihm bin ich es selberin	making it I am (the same as) the promise itself
mein Wort und ich sind eins	my word and I are one
Treue ist wie eine Wurzel	Fidelity is like a root
die hinabreicht bis	that reaches down the ground
ins Grundwasser der ersten Liebe	into the sustaining water of first love
und in dieser Tiefe	and in this depth
Halt und Nahrung findet	finds support and sustenance
wo ich verwurzelt bin	There, where I'm rooted
Da stehe ich.	That's where I stand
und das Gelübde	and the vow
ist kein Konservierungsmittel	is no agent for preservation
vielmehr ein belebendes Ferment	rather it's the enlivening catalyst
das die stets wandelnde Geschichte	that seeks to transform from inside

von innen zu verwandeln sucht	the ever-changing history
durch Sinn und Richtung	giving meaning and direction
damit das Leben nicht	so that life does not fall apart
wie ein zerschellter Krug	like a smashed vessel
in Bruchstücke zerfällt	into tiny pieces
sondern ein Ganzes wird	but that it may become whole
und ich ganz werd in ihm.[14]	and I in it find my wholeness.

In the poem the vow is likened to an invigorating ferment that 'seeks to transform from inside' history with all its instability and vicissitudes. It transforms history by first transforming the individual and this transformation is done *durch Sinn und Richtung,* (through meaning and direction) so that life does not like a smashed jug disintegrate into fragments but that it may become whole. The vow is therefore both active and dynamic and is a catalyst that helps to transform person and history, thereby making life to be integral, complete and perfect. The veracity or the concreteness of such a poem would strike us profoundly if we take time to ask ourselves some basic questions regarding our vows, questions like:

- What does it mean to live the vows; to consecrate my life in the spirit of Poverty, Chastity and Obedience?

- What was it that happened to me on that day when I made my commitment to God in the presence of my community?
- How did I expect my life to change with the commitment?
- Did my life change or is my life changing because of these commitments?
- Am I really closer to God than others are because of this commitment?
- Or rather, was it not a public pledge made to direct my life into a *process* of ever becoming more poor, chaste and obedient?

A sincere personal answer to such questions will throw much light on what the vows are meant to be and not what we ostensibly took them to be. Although they form rules, evangelical counsels are not just only rules, but they are above all art of life and culture of life. They stand for 'greater love' and for 'greater freedom',[15] for growth and development, and that, notwithstanding they also possess 'renunciation' as an undeniable element. The three vows of poverty, chastity and obedience form a single framework of life. It is a way of life defined by the gift of one's life to God in love. The vows open the religious to trust in God's companionship and become the channels of His love. As a choice, the vowed life flows from an experience of being touched in some way by God's loving embrace. They express a desire to allow God's spirit to penetrate every facet of life, and serve as framework not just for living but also for loving. By vows we give our love a future. Love's desire in the vows is more than for the moment. Rather, the vows are a promise that future decisions will be shaped by choices made at the moment. The vows situate religious life as a 'way of living'. While we cannot predict the future, we vow that our decisions will follow a certain path. We limit our freedom and options in order to give our love direction and purpose.

The Three Evangelical Counsels are permanent ways of living out this Consecration. And because they are permanent, they are part and parcel of our daily lives and activities and they express truths that are profoundly rooted into human experience of deeper realities. They therefore need a life programme that should be cultivated. This programme will express itself in:[16]

- a life of personal and communal prayer
- the encounter with the Word of God and the living figure of Christ
- self-knowledge and self-reflection
- fostering community life
- mutual loving, sharing and obeying
- giving Christ to others and encountering Christ in others
- a word, in a 'culture of encounter'[17] of building a better, more just and fraternal world both within

the religious community and in the world at large.

The goal of this programme is to discover joy and fulfilment in one's choice of life. Though on a different note but very pertinent to the religious consecration, Karl Rahner offers a practical guide to these realities that cut deep into the human experience of life, which would help us to cultivate the religious programme. He said:

> Be still for once. Don't try to think of so many complex and varied things. Give … deeper realities of the spirit a chance now to rise to the surface: silence, fear, the ineffable longing for truth, for love, for fellowship, for God. Face loneliness, fear, imminent death! Allow such ultimate, basic human experiences to come first. Don't go talking about them, making up theories about them, but simply endure these basic experiences … If we do not learn slowly in this way to enter more and more into the company of God and to be open to him, if we do not constantly attempt to reflect in life primitive experiences of this kind – not deliberately intended or deliberately undertaken – and from that point onwards to realize them more explicitly in the religious act of meditation and prayer, of solitude and the endurance of ourselves, … then our religious life is and remains really of a secondary character and its conceptual-thematic expression is false.[18]

In the quotation above, Karl Rahner urges us to be still and allow the deeper realities to surface. What are these deeper realities? According to him they are: *silence, fear, loneliness, longing for truth, longing for love and for companionship and above all, longing for God.* He went on to say that we should not make up theories, but rather live it out, experience it, experience ourselves and the other in the depth of who we are. If the promise of the vows is not helping me to experience myself and the other, if it is not helping me to be a real human being capable of experiencing and enduring the basic experiences of life, then my life is a sham. Indeed, it is in living out the realities of the evangelical counsels that these deeper realities of life rise to the surface. Though this fact is true of Christian life in general, it is even more so for the celibate vocation. Quite often, by virtue of the vows, the religious enters into a sort of combat with the self, with silence, fear, the ineffable longing for truth, love, companionship and also for God. When the reality eventually dawns, one sees him/herself facing loneliness, fear, and even imminent death. It is at this point that the 'greater love' and 'greater freedom' which the vows stand for aid the sister/brother to endure these basic experiences.

If we re-consider the quotation from Karl Rahner in the light of Andreas Knapp's poem and the seven basic questions proposed above, the doctrine on the triad could be an enrichment to the theology of religious life but only if they are reviewed, experienced, lived and reconsidered as:

1. *A disposition* which we embrace and which embraces us. Let us not think of the vows as things or actions we promise to do and not to do, to give up, to refrain from or engage in, but we should see them as dispositions. Through the public promises I dispose myself and my entire life to be poor, chaste and obedient.
2. *A way of being*: in which we dwell, as horizons, as depths into which we plunge on a lifelong journey into the silence and the simplicity that is God. Poverty, chastity and obedience, therefore become my lifestyle, my culture of life and my way of life.
3. *Modes of perception*, that is, ways of seeing which enable us to encounter ourselves and the world on a deeper and sacred plane. Frugality of life, purity of life and obedient heart and mind are the compass through which we perceive the world as a whole. Every person and everything have different meanings for us.
4. *A process,* that is, a continuous progression and not the end point of a process. It is an invigorating ferment that bring about an unremitting renewal and an unceasing transformation both internally and externally. In this process of becoming poor, chaste and obedient, I am also aware of my frailty and the sinfulness of human nature. Yet,

confident of the grace of God, the religious are in *via,* on the way. They are certainly not angels, and are unlikely to be so in the short run but they are people who are trying to become religious. The stress falls on '*incessantly trying to become*'.

5. *A spiral,* that is not to be seen as a ladder of perfection, but as a spiral leading into an ever-deepening awareness. A depth experience of the Holy that is all of life with its pains and failures as well as its joys and sacredness as is seen in the whole of creation and which eventually forms a 'whole' wherein I become complete in Him.

When the vows are seen and experienced in the above perspectives, we could then start to speak of life fully lived, of yearnings that lie at the very heart of our humanity. With this, the pronouncing of vows turn out to be a commitment to a *life process*, an unceasing journey into the depths, and a trust-filled movement into possibilities. With this understanding, religious life will no longer be seen as an accomplished fact that identifies us once and for all in a particular state of perfection that can be clearly measured, evaluated and verified through predictable behaviours and which starts on the day of profession.

The Culture of Poverty

The vow of poverty is a religious culture[19] and a definite lifestyle. Going through the history of the consecrated life, we notice that this vow is highly significant, not because it is superior to the vows of chastity and obedience, but because it is the vow which is at the origin of most foundations, reforms, and collapse of religious congregations. It seems that poverty is a kind of thermometer or yardstick for measuring religious congregations. The various interpretations or understandings of poverty became the very source of conflict and disunity within religious orders especially in the Middle Ages among the monks of Cluny and the first generations of the monks of Cîteaux. In the latter part of the 13th century with St Francis of Assisi and his novel and radical interpretation of poverty, the vow of poverty became the litmus test of the fervour and the depth of one's spirituality and of one's dependence on the goodness of God.

Faith is so central in the exercise of obedience; love in chastity; and hope in poverty. Poverty is the easiest of the three vows to comprehend in the sense that the dominant underlying values – sharing, simplicity, responsible stewardship, care and concern for the created order echoes deeply within all people. And all these values are the fruit of one's joyous dependence on God's unfailing love. The truth is that we are all children of the same God and the Creator-God loves everyone in a very unique and personal manner. Everything He has is ours; thus, all the goods of the earth are given by God to all not to be used up abusively but to be used for mutual sustainability, growth and development.

Poverty as a value and a vow is diametrically opposed to the violence of consumerism and deprivation. God the Creator is pleased to see that no one suffers from want and insufficiency because of the greed of the powerful, for He has blessed the earth with more than enough goods to sustain life. Poverty, however is not destitution.

The primary motive for embracing voluntarily the vow of poverty is not to enter into solidarity with those who have nothing. The primary reason is love. Our identification with the poor is a consequence and not the primary reason. The motive is Jesus Christ, who calls us in love to respond to His love for us. This loving response made by the power of his spirit, leads us to live out religious poverty after his imitation. It associates us with Jesus who lived poor and died without anything, without material possessions and who died stripped of all honour, dignity and respect. It associates us intimately with Jesus in His passion and death, crucifying us to the world and the world to us (Galatians 6:14). It frees us from the ambition for honours, for applause and even for being deemed holy. This Christological sense of poverty has as its real Benedictine name '*humilitas*'; not the moral virtue of humility but rather the path trod by Christ himself, the paschal virtue of abasement, which the follower of Christ does by total dis-appropriation. This abasement is more than simple material poverty, as it empties the religious, in the sense of a *kenosis*, of everything that is his/her own; his/her will, his/her body, and the material goods he/she uses.[20] It is at this deep Christological level that poverty and obedience meet, in which the voluntary displacement of Christ who abases himself in his obedience to the Father and who stripped himself of equality with him are seen.

It is in this Christological sense that the real spirit of poverty is to be found, while its practical applications to the individual or collective dealings with material goods may differ from time to time. For example when we say that through the vow of poverty the religious is in solidarity with the poor, the interpretative meaning of such solidarity has been carried out in vast different ways. St Francis and the Franciscans for example preferred to share poverty with the poor themselves, through a radical emptying-out of self, a *kenosis*; while St Benedict and the Benedictines understood this as sharing the monastery's property with the poor, to alleviate their needs and afford them relief.

Poverty grants the freedom one needs in order to be disposed to receive things gratefully and be able to share. The sharing at this level includes not only sharing of goods but also the sharing of other values as well. It is expected from every human being to act and make choices and decisions, not out of one's need but out of one's value. Poverty becomes an interior attitude, a witness to our interior values. Central to the evangelical counsel of poverty is the fact that it is a free choice. It is a situation, an art or a culture of life into which one grows deeper and deeper and not a condition against which one must fight to liberate oneself.[21] That is why it is part of the programme for the voluntary displacement in following the displaced Lord. Even though poverty may involve giving away everything, its very first duty, however, consists in receiving everything, that is to say, its first dynamics is not expropriation but grateful possession. This is seen in the fact that I am not master/mistress of my life, but rely on and receive from others – without being able to compensate immediately, perhaps without ever being able to pay back. This is the difficult part of any form of poverty. The evangelical poverty invariably puts the religious on the receiving end of life, between God and the human beings through whom God let the religious receive and experience his providential care. A yes to this nature of poverty also means a reconciled yes to myself, to my human history, to my limits and to the injuries inflicted on my life.

The Three Dimensions of Poverty

The vow of poverty is not primarily about renouncing things. The vow is something interior and spiritual – not something easily quantifiable or measurable. It is primarily about our relationship with God, with others and things. The first dimension of poverty concerns our *relationship with God*. This vow makes no sense if one is not passionately in love with Christ. He becomes the pearl of great price that one loves and that one is prepared to posses by leaving all things behind (cf. Matthew 13:46). In studying His life in the Scriptures, we find that Christ, far from renouncing life, instead celebrated it. The first manifestation of his Divine power was in changing water into wine (John 2:1-11) wherein the Bible says he revealed his glory. Christ came eating and drinking and his opponents accused Him of being a glutton and a drunkard. We know that Christ is the vine and we, who are his, are the branches (John.15:1-11). By transforming the water into wine, Christ demonstrated that He indeed is the true vine. The servants were also able to produce wine by abiding in Christ as exemplified in the fact that they did what he asked them to do. If Christ is the gem of our life we shall never lack anything and our poverty would be fruitful.

This leads to the second level of the vow of poverty: *our relationship with others*. The vow of poverty makes the most sense when lived in a religious community. The religious communities should live as Jesus and His disciples lived. They held a common purse, and their needs were provided for from the common purse. They were neither destitute nor obsessed with personal comfort. Also the vow of poverty is an invitation to be there for others. It is not natural to live one's life for others. Most men only learn to turn from selfishness and self-centeredness by having a wife and children for whom to care. In the religious life, this vow is what helps turn us away from our innate self-centred and self-seeking inclination. No longer obsessed with our own needs, we can more readily focus on the needs of others, including those whose needs are the greatest. Along the way, we awaken to the reality that we are richly provided for by Christ.

The third level of this vow concerns *our relationship to things*. We learn, like St Paul, the secret of enjoying abundance and of being content with very little. That is the lesson that the vow of poverty teaches us. For one who is vowed to poverty, each day slowly becomes enough. We learn anew how to enjoy life as when we were little children. When our vision is clear, we even learn to appreciate what is ugly and unpleasant.

Since we live in a world with abundant resources made available for the benefit of everyone by God in His divine providence, could we not satisfy the needs of all if we control our desire to possess and consume? We hope that our witness to poverty, confirmed by our vow, can say something to the world about dependence on God, the joy of sharing, solidarity with the poor and the structural changes that would resolve many of the problems of our contemporary world. Fidelity to and perseverance in these three levels of living the spirit of poverty after the example of Christ free us gradually from attachment to places, ministries, material possessions and self-centeredness. It makes us capable of viewing all good things as God's gifts and of living in gratitude for what we have received. It liberates us, so that we recognize the generous hand of God in all that happens, seeing his love in every person; thus it enables us to love in a new way. If we truly give ourselves over to the life of the evangelical counsels, we will find it possible to use things in the light of their relation to the Kingdom of God. We will be free to move wherever the demands of the mission indicate and the Spirit calls.

Community Dimension of Religious Poverty

When we talk of the vow of poverty making us to be at the receiving end of life we should know that this is true thanks to the providence of God through the community, whose life we share. Like the other counsels, religious poverty (vow of poverty) also has a community dimension. It springs from the truth that religious profession expresses the gift of self to God and to the Church, a gift that is lived within the community of a religious family. Religious are not only called to an individual personal vocation. Their call is also a *convocation* with others with whom they share their daily lives. That is why a religious cannot pretend not to care about what the other brother/sister does with his/her life. Religious life obliges one to care and to be our 'brother's keeper'. It is my responsibility to see to it that my fellow brother/sister is living out his/her religious vows. This I have to do by being conscious of my own life, living an exemplary life. The members are congregated, united together into a single community by their 'yes' to follow the poor, obedient and chaste Christ. They are united with Christ, and therefore called to be united among themselves. They are united in the mission to prophetically oppose the idolatry of power, of possessions, and of pleasure. They are bonded by the same intention, the same *charism*, and the same love for God. Poverty, the sharing of goods, even spiritual goods, has been from the beginning the basis of fraternal communion. The poverty of individual members, which brings with it a simple and austere lifestyle, not only frees them from concerns inherent in private ownership but it also enriches the community, enabling it to serve God and the poor more effectively. A community/institute is truly living the spirit of poverty if the individual member is living it, too. At the economic level, the poorer the individual member is, the richer the community/institute becomes. The richer the individual, the poorer the institute is. From the very beginning of religious life, evangelical poverty and a common life with shared material things began to be closely associated. So it is that community life is central and important in living out the vows especially the vows of Chastity and Poverty.

The Wealth of Poverty

In spite of the renouncing aspect of poverty a religious is a wealthy person, in as much as he/she possesses Christ. We have our Lord's words for it that 'those who have left mother, father, brother and sister for my sake and for the sake of the Gospel shall receive a hundredfold in this life and in the next life eternal' (Matthew 19:29; Mark 10:28-30; Luke 18:29). Again, when St Paul speaks of having nothing yet possessing all things (2 Corinthians 6:10), he describes total detachment, which covers a wider area than that of religious poverty. He was referring to an ideal state of mind towards which this poverty should lead and guide the religious. Gerard Mackrell narrated a beautiful story, which brings out clearly the meaning of this Pauline passage. He said:

> I was waiting to cross a busy road at the side of which were parked a gleaming, expensive car, a young boy, and myself. After gazing furtively around him the child walked up to the car and touched it with such a reverence. At that moment the owner of the vehicle materialised from the nearby expensive-looking house and he told the boy to go away. The man then asked me if I was surprised at his annoyance. On my not answering, he added: 'That kid is here every day, and gets more pleasure from the car than I do. And I bought the thing.'[22]

You see, the car was a 'thing' to the owner, who was jealous of the boy's pleasure. In a sense the boy was more an owner of the car than the purchaser. For the latter it was either a status symbol, or a means of conveyance, or something to unload his money onto;

for the boy who stared at it with eyes wide as saucers it was something rapturous, and that rapture no man could take from him. In this sense, we can own everything: sun, moon, and untold splendour while remaining penniless. The greatest asset we possess is a meaning to life, that not only do we have something to live for, but that our life is full of purpose: we understand what life is all about and above all possess Life who is Christ Himself.

The vow of poverty is not in fact about external poverty, it is not necessarily the absence of possessions. It is rather not being possessed by anything, be it money or other worldly belongings. It is being free from what is 'mine', being able to say the prayer of Jesus fully: that which is mine is yours and that which is yours is mine (John 17:10). It is recognizing that 'the earth is the Lord's and the fullness thereof: the world, and they that dwell therein' (Psalms 24:1). It is being able really and truly to live the Eucharistic prayer which the Church assembled offers at every Divine Liturgy in the Eastern rite, right after the *epiclesis*: 'Thine own, out of Thine own, we offer to Thee entirely and for all things'. He who seeks to be poor in this sense understands the meaning of *kenosis,* the self-emptying of God in the incarnation: 'though he was rich, yet … he became poor, that we through his poverty might be rich' (2 Corinthians 8:9). Therefore poverty is an emptying of oneself for others in the likeness of the Lord,[23] so that we might rightly have a share in his richness.

The Culture of Chastity

The culture of chastity is one of the oldest and the most enduring of all the vows. It is unique among the vows professed by the Religious. This is so because it is the only vow whose content has been a constant factor in all forms of religious life throughout history. It is also the only one of the three vows whose object is, strictly speaking, 'an evangelical counsel' in the sense that it is a response to an invitation not addressed to all Christians. So it can be taken as the defining characteristic of religious life. Moreover, it is viewed as a commitment of love and not just a renunciation of marriage and sexual gratification.

The word chastity is from Latin *castus,* meaning 'chaste', 'pure'. It is a *process* of *becoming*; nothing is just 'pure' but it becomes pure.

> *Castus* was the word the overseer used when his slaves had finished scrubbing the marble floors at the crack of dawn each morning, having reported to the mistress that the floors had been scrubbed and hence were clean, the mistress then proceeded with affairs of the household. It is important to note that *castus* not only denotes the accomplished fact of cleanliness, but it also denotes that it was a cleanliness achieved by the *process* of scrubbing. It is that awareness of a *process,* not in itself an end, but aiming towards an end more important than the act by which the end is realized and through which it

> is attained. Applied to the concept of chastity, it is to be noted that the *process* of cleansing is not only apropos of the end, but necessary to it.[24]

So opting for the vow of chastity one pledges oneself into this *dynamic process* of daily 'scrubbing' and daily struggle to be pure. It is a process that involves the whole person but which has a seat in the human heart. The heart is the seat of chastity. Defining celibacy, Richard Sipe wrote: 'Religious celibacy is a *freely chosen, dynamic state*, usually vowed, that involves *an honest and sustained attempt* to live without direct sexual gratification in order to serve others productively for a spiritual motive.'[25]

Chastity or rather celibacy is *dynamic*; it is a *process* of internalization and actualization of the celibate ideal from intention to achievement. Chastity does not ordinarily begin with practice, but with the formation of an image of chastity, often personified in one person believed to be chaste, or in a programme of life as some have in the novitiate formation. This *process* involves the achievement of a degree of self-knowledge, measuring one's own capacity to live with the sexual discipline and deprivation necessary to be chaste or celibate. The novitiate formative years thus provide measuring periods for such knowledge of oneself. Having some degree of self-awareness readies a person to proceed further in seeking knowledge about the *process* of chastity and what it involves in realistic terms. Because chastity is neither abstract nor extraneous to the individual striving for it, these inevitable steps, or inevitable stages in formation precede the experimentation, the practice and eventually the total commitment of one's life into it. If, in time, chastity takes personal root, it is often capped by a formal vow, the vow of chastity. It is from a stable internal base that chastity can be said to reach achievement once its integration is woven into the fibre of one's being. That is when chastity becomes an integral part of one's sexual self. Self-revelation of such a *process* is never simple.[26]

However, those who understand chastity to mean simply bodily chastity fall into the error common in western thought of dissociating body from soul. In fact the East does not know any such distinction. It talks about the human person, not about a soul-body dichotomy. The vow of chastity is therefore primarily chastity of thought (thinking no evil), of the heart (bearing no evil for anyone), of the tongue (speaking no evil), of the ears (not willing to listen to false accusations against anyone), and of the eyes (not coveting, seeing no evil). Bodily chastity then follows. It is striving to recapture in the 'not-yet', the full manifestation of the Kingdom when the whole of creation is restored to its virginity.[27] The importance of purity of heart – which is chastity of the heart, of thought, of the tongue, ears, eyes and so on – in the practising of the virtue of chastity cannot be overemphasized, for 'purity of heart is the absolute foundation for a chaste life. Only one who is moving towards singleness of purpose will have the courage to pursue the virtue, despite temptation and failure.'[28]

Chastity is the Vow of the Heart – Love

The central organ in living out the vow of chastity is the heart and not necessarily the body. Once the heart is properly channelled the body automatically follows as a matter consequence. It must be stressed that chastity is above all else a matter of the heart. By vowing chastity, the religious has done so much more than promise not to marry or to have a family; he/she has promised to keep his/her love for God, neighbour, and to live with a generous heart. We have promised not to hold our heart in reserve for certain experiences or just a few close relationships, for Jesus certainly did not. Jesus gave freely of His heart entering into every human struggle, including the struggle of surrender to the will of His Father. We have promised to pray from the heart. More than simply choosing not to give our hearts to another in marriage or to have any other human being as the centre of our lives, we have chosen to give our heart to God in imitation of Jesus who poured forth His heart to the Father in prayer. By the vow of chastity we are called not just to pray, but to pray like Jesus did, from the depths of our hearts. We have promised to live from the heart, giving and receiving hospitality by situating every relationship in our lives within our relationship to God. Jesus lived an expansive and gracious hospitality, welcoming everyone He encountered into the heart of His relationship with God. We are called to live with a hospitable heart open to receiving and giving ourselves to others. By our vow of chastity we desire to reflect God's love for us by a faithful and loving relationship with friends and companions in the community and seek to live in single-hearted intimacy with God. By so doing we vow to live in awareness of the deepest desires that God has placed within our hearts. If one struggles to live out this vow, one finds out that the living of this vow invites one into a whole series of interrelated and dynamic relationships that demand the fullness of one's heart.

If we all agree up till this point that the vow of chastity is the vow of the heart then it logically follows that it is the vow of love: love of God and love of neighbour, therefore affective and effective love is the centre of this vow. The vow of chastity is a call from God to love: to love more, to love better and to love universally. The religious, like any other person, is called to integrate the various human dimensions of life. He/she has not given up the need to love and be loved, nor his human affectivity or sexuality. No one can renounce generativeness and the need to be creative. The vow instead excludes certain ways of expressing these basic human needs, but, precisely because of this exclusion, it also requires other expressions: friendship and the community are the two privileged areas for discovering healthy ways of expressing and receiving love and for integrating sexuality and affectivity maturely into a harmonious life project. Ministry and service are appropriate fields for creativity and generativeness.

Means to Grow in the Dynamic Process *of being Chaste*

There are so many means available for growth in the virtue of chastity but we have to single out six important means. These five are extracted from the experience of deeper realities of which Karl Rahner spoke above, for it is by experiencing to the full these human realities of life that one grows in chastity.

1. *Community Life:* Celibate chastity is the primary vow of the community because by in it we embrace a disposition of trust and of vulnerability, of surrender to love each other. It is an ideal towards which we vow our life. The living of celibate chastity is a lifelong task. It is not an accomplished fact on the day of profession; instead it is a *process*, a movement, a hope to render to Christ recognition that in Him we live and have our being. That I have chosen as a celibate not to express my love genitally does not mean that I do not or I should not express my love. Unfortunately, in our world of today, to love means to be genitally involved and this is what we should contradict by our vow of Chastity. One who is chaste becomes progressively warmer and more loving. Love

is the virtue of a chaste person, contrary to what people believe. It is the experience of many that good friendships and the benefit of living in a warm and supportive community are normal conditions for both faithfulness and perseverance in living a chaste life. One cannot survive without some sense of closeness and if a religious community does not provide this, it is then not surprising that its members will find themselves more attractive elsewhere.[29]

There are three basic qualities in celibate chastity which community life helps to foster:

a) *Disposition*: My disposition in my community needs to be one of openness on initial contact with each individual in the community. One who enters religious life carries with him/her the burden of his/her past which in philosophy is called *'facticity'*.[30] We bring what Barbara Fiand would call 'our prison walls'[31] and they are often unconscious and it is good for us to know that all of us have 'prison walls' and for most of us it is unconscious. And those with whom we relate and interact encounter us also out of their *facticity*, i.e. out of their own 'prison walls'. So their openness is not the openness of the glass; it is human openness, with human frailty and a human past. That is to say that their openness is often clouded with unconscious projections and unacknowledged expectations. This initial disposition and the consciousness of our unconscious *facticity* is a good step towards letting life be permeated by the love of the community and my acceptance of being vulnerable in their midst.

b) *Interaction*: In interaction we stretch out to each other, care for, as well as hurt each other. Through our constant day-to-day community living and frequent meetings with our individual brokenness, individual unconscious baggage, we begin to project and eventually our trust might turn into distrust. We feel rejection, pain and we are wounded. It is here that our vow of chastity enters into the picture of that mercy situation. In interaction we embrace the flood of life to which we have committed ourselves by this form of relationship with all its anguish, turmoil and all its grace. We allow ourselves to endure it all, be with it and let it teach us. We do not run away from this flood of pain nor do we busy ourselves with only ministerial work but we immerse ourselves into a deepened attitude of openness and of trust-grown-wiser. This eventually will lead us into the third attitude.

c) *Deepened disposition*: this will make us walk in this earth compassionately. It is at this level that we become really Christ's disciples who are likened to their Master with a compassionate heart for the sinned-against. At this level we are ready for love. Having met, and continued to meet our own 'noonday devil' and knowing how weak we are, we support others in their own brokenness and we thereby learn how to love. That is why Barbara Fiand said, that Celibacy is a commitment to live life fully with its pains and with its ecstasy. When we promise celibate chastity we say: 'I promise to journey into the agony and the ecstasy of relationship, into the turmoil, the pain and revelation of myself to myself, of others and of God which loving non-possessively will open up for me.'[32]

2. *Asceticism and discipline:* They are very necessary in living out a chaste and consecrated love by overcoming all forms of egoistic tendencies and subjective values. *Vita Consecrata,* 38 says: 'Asceticism, by helping to master and correct the inclinations of human nature wounded by sin, is truly indispensable if consecrated persons are to remain faithful to their own vocation and follow Jesus on the way of the Cross.' Renunciation of one value is necessary in order to grow on a higher value. 'While sexual desire is a natural drive it also raises natural resistances. Self-control or self-mastery is one of the essential developmental life tasks. Athletic, intellectual, or military conquests as well as religious idealism all depend for success on the drive to conquer one's self and modulate natural desires.'[33] Asceticism, self-control and self-mastering are all necessary for any meaningful achievement in life and more so for spiritual life. However, 'Celibacy is unlike other modes of asceticism – fasting, sleep deprivation, endurance of extreme temperatures, or even poverty – in that sexual pleasure or activity is not necessary for

individual survival as are some measure of sustenance, recuperation, and protection from the elements. These modes of controlling natural desires have often been used as adjunctive, supportive, and protective of the dedicated celibate's pursuit of his or her goal.'[34]

3. *Solitude:* Solitude is an indispensable element in order to find oneself, integrate those aspects and levels of self, which are troublesome, and have an identity, a personal identity in Christ, which can be offered as gifts to others. Desert experiences lead a person into contact with the basic essential needs, values, attitudes of the self; they help confront a person with love and give time to work through a proper integration. We need the silence of solitude to be with our Spouse, to find the hurts and fears, the uncertainty and pain, as well as the joy and peace, desire and gratitude. It is at the same time very therapeutic and a challenge to firmly and courageously face ourselves. It is in solitude that the deeper realities Karl Rahner spoke of above, become fully experienced. He said: 'be still for once. Don't try to think of so many complex and varied things. Give deeper realities of the spirit chance to rise to the surface, endure these basic experiences'.[35] In a word he is saying 'try to enter into solitude', because it is in solitude that one is able to enter more and more into the company of God and be open to him and to his transforming action.

Solitude is the context and opportunity to assimilate

and integrate what God is saying to me in both my prayer life and in my interaction with others. It is the moment of holding together diverse experiences, with their possibilities and contradictions, while awaiting the birth of new insight, new intuition, new challenge, and a new sense of being called forth in the service of the Kingdom. Furthermore, solitude allows the religious to give space and time to 'come home to oneself, to tune in to the God within, the source of our living water welling up in the heart.'[36] It is in solitude that one is able to discover oneself and God. As Krenik writes, 'deep within each person is a '*celibate core*', a '*sacred centre*' that no other human person touches. This is where the spirit of God dwells. It is a place of naked solitude. It is the inward desert where we grapple with our demons and dark night; it is the place where God purifies our hearts and transforms our desires.'[37] The internal vacuum created by the loneliness of celibate life could be a fertile ground for nurturing unfathomable behaviours. When solitude is 'boldly and courageously faced and embraced, the egotistical deception of false unity, false security, and false relationship are dismantled to reveal the ultimate and final celibate option: surrendering to the terrible oneness of the God of infinite mystery, the unknown and unknowable God of infinite possibility.'[38]

4. *Service:* Service is love in action. It is a genuine way of renewing, preserving and augmenting one's love.

It is a way of bringing the fruits of solitude back to try them in reality. It is also a test of our love. Living our vow of chastity is something serious, deep, and challenging. We can and should seek to respond to that challenge and in a renewed way, to love chastity as Christ loves, to surrender our body, our spiritual needs to intimacy with Him, to His heart, to enter into His love, to open and to abandon ourselves to it. There are certain qualities that measure the authenticity of a chaste life: these are service, awareness of the oneness of the human condition and the capacity to love.[39]

5. *Prayer – Meditation: Vita Consecrata,* 38 says: 'Prayer is the best weapon we can have against all sorts of temptations that beset us. In practice this involves great fidelity to liturgical and personal prayer, to periods devoted to mental prayer and contemplation, to Eucharistic adoration, to monthly retreats and to spiritual exercises.' It is the lifeblood of our ministry and apostolate and a means of deepening our friendship with God. The Gospels are the best source of our meditation and prayer. Our capacities to relate to the self and to others also determine the quality of our relationship with God. Prayer is a communication, which brings about a corresponding quality of relationship. So the quality of our relationship mirrors the quality of our prayer life.

The practice of prayer and humility, love of others expressed in service and generosity to them, solitude, asceticism and discipline, the whole sense of discipleship are strengths which flow into chastity.

The Culture of Obedience

The term 'obedience' is derived from the Latin *oboedire* which literally means listening; that is, to listen intently, to open one's ears, to heed in practice. As we know from Isaiah 55:11, God's word is not merely an expression of His will but also its execution. Hence listening includes doing. The word is not heard if it is not executed (Luke 6:46-47; 11:28). Such is the obedience that constitutes Christian discipleship and guarantees almost a blood relationship with Jesus (Matthew 12:48-49). Obedience is an attitude of attentiveness and responsiveness to the call of the moment that originates from the internal and external forces. It is not 'primarily a submission to laws. … It is life lived with the alertness of the Spirit, attentiveness to things that really matter.'[40] The culture of obedience demands that one places oneself in an atmosphere of openness and faithfulness 'to God, to others, to life's circumstances, to nature, to the many calls of daily living, and to respond in a manner that enhances growth.'[41]

By its very nature, religious obedience is primarily and essentially the obedience of Jesus Christ to the Father whose goal is to be intimately united with Him. It is a deepening of Christian obedience with Christ as the point of reference and identification. Through religious profession of the vow, it becomes more binding and more intense in terms of its praxis. Besides, it is being lived within the ambience of a particular institute that has a specific *charism*, lifestyle, vision, and mission. Rule and/or Constitutions must also be considered in every decision-making, project and activity.

The obedience of Christ has specific characteristics inherent to it. It is a free and loving adherence to the salvific plan of God who sent Him for a purpose. In his very words, 'I seek not to do my own will but the will of Him who sent me.' (John 5:30) Jesus' obedience can be said to have a triple dimension: It is a *relationship*, which implies a faithful listening, and an adherence to God's Word, through which Jesus came to know the fact that He is the Son; as a *following or doing of God's will,* which Jesus expresses as His meat and drink; and as a *mission* which is the sense of being 'sent' to bring about the Kingdom.[42]

Christ's threefold Obedience

As a relationship with God the Father: Jesus' obedience was the fruit of His intimate friendship with the Father. He loved to go to isolated places to pray and commune with the Father. Prayer became the lifeblood of His ministry. He lived in constant company with Him who sent Him, listening to His words, discerning His loving will, and carrying it out. The strength and energy which He drew from His silent moments with the Father sustained Him in trials. Hence in Hebrews

5:8, we learnt that the oppositions Jesus encountered in being faithful to God actually bound Him closer to God.[43] The obedience of Jesus is a total *kenosis,* a self-emptying. Thus, 'He emptied Himself and took the form of a slave and became obedient unto death, even death on the cross' (Philippians 2:7).

As a doing of the Father's will: Doing God's will is a decision accompanied by a series of continuous choices. This is made clear by Jesus in John 7:17, 'If anyone chooses to do God's will, he will find out whether my teaching comes from God or whether I speak on my own'. Note the first part of that statement: 'If anyone chooses to do God's will'. It helps us to understand that we can make a choice in our lives to do God's will. It is not a one-time decision alone. But it is a choice that has to be made again and again. These are choices that strengthen one's decision to do God's will. In this light, examining Jesus' statement: 'For I have come down from heaven not to do my will but to do the will of him who sent me' (John 6:38), it is interesting to note that Jesus also had to choose the right decision each time He was offered a different option. For example, when Peter tried to turn Him away from the suffering of the cross, Jesus rebuked Peter and chose the cross (Matthew 16:23). And at the Garden of Gethsemane, even though He was in intense agony, He chose to drink the cup of the suffering of the cross and obey His Father's will (Matthew 26:39, 42, 44). Thus, even for Jesus, doing

God's will required a continuous choice in life. In John 4:34, Jesus made it clear that his food is to do God's will. Thus Christ's obedience was voluntary (will), active (intelligence), and responsible (decision). It is true that self-denial and renunciation of one's own will are elements of religious obedience but these must not be the focus.

The desire to please God was a dominant force in the life of Jesus. Jesus once said: 'The one who sent me is with me; he has not left me alone, *for I always do what pleases him*' (John 8:29). Jesus enjoyed a continuous conscious presence of God his Father in His life because He always did what pleased God. Therefore, Jesus was never in doubt as to what the will of his Father was, because his obedience was motivated by love. For He says, 'The world must know that I love the Father and that I do just as the Father has commanded me.' (John 14:31). So also religious life has its ultimate and most profound purpose and meaning in love. Its highest mission is to prove this love in the test of obedience. On the most exalted level, love and obedience are one.

As part of his mission: As we saw in chapter one of this work on Jesus' religious identity; he received a mission from the Father (Luke 4:16-18) and lived as an obedient apostle to the will of the Father (John 4:34; 10:36; 20:21; Hebrews 3:1). In his faithfulness to this mission received, he had concern for those outside the margins of social acceptance. Thus, his mission involved forgiveness, compassion, table-fellowship with sinners and traitors, in a word, to the sinned-against. 'He proclaimed the Kingdom and was made real through His own activity as healer, exorcist and preacher.'[44] This implies a preferential option for the sinned-against as they were in different categories; the lost, the least, the lasts; for the unlovable, the unloving, and the unloved sectors of the society. But it does not mean an exclusive love for them alone, for Christ's love is inclusive. Christ's authority was based on his involvement with such people because he was aware that that was the Father's will.

Religious Obedience as a Daily Task and a Daily Yes

This vow, like the other two, cuts deep. Being obedient is a daily task. There are innumerable experiences – from simple community duties like washing dishes to confronting global issues such as poverty and the world – that provoke our response as religious. In fact, I have come to ponder on the complexity of the vow, of its all-inclusive nature. How is it possible to be obedient in such a profound way to God's will? The answer, as found in the Gospels, is simple: one step at a time. When Christ talks of the coming Kingdom, we hear of the lilies of the field, the mustard seed so small that its size betrays its enormous potentials, the grain of wheat whose death is only a step towards nourishment and life. These images tell us that our conformity to God's will – the bending and shaping and reforming of our ego's desires to what obedience calls forth from us – is a slow, cumbersome, and occasionally painful process. And yet, in becoming a sown grain of wheat or a mustard seed planted in fertile soil, we learn that obedience moves us beyond our enthusiastic 'yes' or a fearful 'why' to a simple embrace of Christ Himself. That is because, in the end, we are obedient not out of fear or duty, but simply out of love of God who first loved us.

Obedience: A Relationship with the persona Christi

The vow of obedience goes beyond superior/subject link of giving command and obeying the command, to creating a specific relationship, a relationship of submission, reverence and love between the religious and the person of Christ, a relationship of submission that goes beyond the obligation of doing what the superior commands or the general obligations of any law (the rule of the congregation, Constitutions and directories). It is the placing of one's whole life, activity and destiny at God's disposal in a very real and concrete way. Just because the very purpose of this vow is a *relationship* of a more total surrender and availability to Christ, religious obedience therefore is an end in itself: it is given for the sake of obedience and surrender itself. 'We vow obedience for one fundamental reason: to be more really and completely surrendered to the person of Jesus Christ.'[45]

Even when it comes to its apostolic aspect, i.e.

obedience of mission, the vow is not measured by the demands of some concrete mission or apostolate to be accomplished or some corporate unity to be achieved. Rather, the vow establishes one in a state of total availability to Christ, and of desired union with his will, so that one can be used in every way that leads directly or indirectly to the realization of the Kingdom of God. This availability is total as we saw in Christ who lived as an obedient apostle to the will of the Father. Then the 'Kingdom of God' which we are talking about is not a concrete task to be accomplished on earth in the sense of something that can be produced by human efforts; rather it is the total subordination of all things to Christ the Head, as Christ himself is subordinated to God the Father. Obedience, then, in a sense is that Kingdom. This explains why the obedience of mission does not stop at chores like the building and staffing of schools, the burden of teaching, preaching, serving the sick and poor, or altering social structures and so on. Religious obedience is not just a practical means to doing these things more efficiently and well. The mission to which religious obedience consecrates us is that of 'restoring all things in Christ' (Ephesians 1:10) within ourselves and in others, and our first step in this direction is the vow that puts our own persons in a real relationship of total submission to Christ through a submission to human superiors that aims at being as total as possible.[46] The theological foundation of religious obedience is a faith-vision that sees in the person of the superior (or in the community, should that be the case) as Christ in *persona* made present: commanding, inviting, and receiving service, obedience, reverence, and love.

Obedience is desirable as a state of *being, a lifestyle*, an atmosphere where one moves and grows, and not as a means to getting some job done; and therefore the 'need' for such an obedience is not measured by function, practicality nor by capability. In this sense, obedience is similar to contemplation because it is not a motion towards something, a motion that is finished when its object is attained; rather, it is a *relationship* with God that in a sense is never completely attained, because it is the subjecting of all of one's being to all of His desire. It is a state of being desired for its own sake, which when attained will simply endure and intensify itself.[47]

How does the person of the human superior fit into such a relationship?

The key to this relationship with God is the correlation that one freely accepts and establishes by vow with a concrete human authority ordinarily vested in the person of a superior. The person of this human authority with all limitations and finitude makes it that the *raison d'être* of this vow is deeply rooted in faith, for without faith one can never live the vow of obedience. It is faith based on doing everything in the name of the Lord Jesus (Colossians 3:17) and on the belief that the superior or the community commands in the place and in the name of God.

The Present Situation

The complexity of modern life gives rise to a new environment for living evangelical obedience. There is a growing awareness of the value of the human person and the rights of individuals. We are more and more conscious of the importance of self-expression and the need to participate in the decisions that affect our lives. Everywhere people demand respect for different opinions, ideas, cultures and practices and expect the right to question or criticize authority. The principle of subsidiarity, recognizing the legitimate autonomy of individuals and of institutions, has taken on new importance as autocratic methods give way to democratic styles of governing in society. The pyramidal conception of the Church, wherein authority descends from above hierarchically down and those at the top have a special connection with the divine, thereby giving the people command or absolutely detecting for them the will of God, gives way to the Church as a circle, where the members are holding hands together and whoever is the superior extends his/her hands to his/her brothers and sisters: all together in dialogue and participation discern the will of God for the individuals and for the group. Moreover, even though these ideas are frequently honoured more in theory than in practice, they still form the basis for contemporary thinking.

There is, however, a negative side to this reality: a distorted sense of personal liberty, which highlights rights and downplays responsibilities, fosters egoism and an atmosphere of exaggerated individualism. Abuse of power, expressed in the betrayal of public trust or in a lack of respect for human rights, or even direct oppression, has led some to view authority with suspicion and others to adopt a lifeless passivity before authority. Religious congregations and communities, of course, have not remained unaffected by contemporary developments in society. Adequate steps should be taken in promoting dialogue and participation in community decisions. In this sense obedience should be lived in a spirit of mutual responsibility.

Another problem today facing religious congregations is the expansion of the Congregation into different parts of the world where there are very distinct cultures and where different concepts of authority confront and dialogue with one another. This produces some tension between western notions of obedience and the ways other cultural traditions come to decisions. Much sensitivity will be needed to discover how best to understand the essential meaning of obedience in these new situations.

Listening and Dialogue foster Obedience

Today, the vow of obedience is a means to develop the Religious as adults. Structures of obedience in the community such as communal discernment, congregational processes, and roles of authority call the religious to both obey authority and participate in authority.[48] The Church is indeed dynamic, growing, and open to changes and renewal. 'The effort to build communities that are less formalistic, less authoritarian, more fraternal and participatory, is generally considered to be one of the visible fruits of these recent years.'[49] In this wise, it is important to remember that the Spirit of God speaks through all, and even more concretely 'the Lord often reveals what is better to the younger' (RB 3:3). Authority in the Congregation/community which is a function of seeking and acting on God's will, should be undertaken in a spirit of dialogue and consultation. The wisdom in dialogue and seeking counsel is not a contemporary discovery or invention even though our situation today absolutely calls for it. The proof of this fact is that St Benedict in the fifth century writing a rule for his monks, wisely added that the Abbot should do all things with the counsel of the brethren and encourage every member of the community to 'express their opinions with all humility, and not presume to defend their own views obstinately' (RB 3:4). Superiors have the delicate task of promoting the discernment of God's will and the ultimate responsibility for decision-making. 'They should engage in dialogue', but they 'retain the authority to decide and command what is to be done' (RB 3:5; Can 97 § 2).

Since ordinarily we know God's will through human mediation, obedience demands a process of discernment. The religious needs to listen to God's voice not only in his/her own heart; he/she must at the same time, pay attention to how God speaks through the needs of the poor, the signs of the times, in the Church, in the events of the world, in the community, and in the directives of legitimate authority. Attentive listening is a *community project* which summons all to dialogue in sincerity as brothers/sisters and to search together for God's will. Obedience also demands that, after dialogue, implementation through concrete projects and actions of what is perceived as God's will becomes necessary. We hope that our obedience can say something to the world about listening to each other, about dialogue, respecting differences of opinion and culture, and the need to work together in cooperation. It is in this sense of dialogical interdependence that the person at the head becomes a channel for the individual personal encounter and relationship with the *persona Christi.*

At the core of Jesus' redemptive mission lies his unconditional obedience to the Father. This filial obedience is the immediate consequence of a life totally given over to the Kingdom of God. Christ's obedience is *passive* in the sense that he submits to the human condition and accepts suffering and death. But it is, above all, *active* because he consistently offers himself to do his Father's will. A human lifestyle which consists in the free subordination to something higher than itself cannot exist without an element of risk. 'And without such a surrender the individual will remain in his own egotism behind the defences of his own existential anxiety, which is the surest way to destruction. But the man who gives himself to what is higher and nobler, who takes the gamble, knows that he is only doing what Christ Himself did in His obedience.'[50] So the passive and active dimensions of Christ' obedience are a gamble which the religious by vowing obedience has willingly accepted to play with his/her life.

However, the freedom that comes from such a gamble; identifying ourselves fully with God's point of view makes obedience *prophetic*. When fidelity to God becomes our principal motivation, all our other motives and plans become subordinate. Obedience should be capable of challenging not only our own personal desires and goals, but those of the larger society as well. Under this aspect, Karl Rahner is of the opinion that 'that which in a given instance is irrational and indefensible but actually unavoidable really becomes the will of the Father. In this way the cross of Christ, a crime of the Jews and the pagans, "had" to be; it was the will of the Father who had planned it, even though it came about only as the result of the short-sightedness and guilt of men.'[51]

That is to say that 'obedience must be regarded as the will of God, even if a particular command appears to be senseless (just as death, failure and the other tragic circumstances of human existence appear), provided of course that what is commanded is not immoral in itself. Religious obedience is thus a real participation in the cross of Christ. Nor should one protest that the irrationality of a mistaken command frees the subject from his contract, and cannot be considered as a share in Christ's mission.'[52]

No to Absoluteness and One-sidedness of the Vows

The Vow seen and lived as a *process* of becoming should be able to possess the inherent power of saying No to idolization of the evangelical counsels and be capable of pointing to the greater reality. There are instances where certain aspects of life according to the evangelical counsels are absolutely set and their relatedness to a broader reality is no longer significant. Examples are:

- When the instrumental character of the vows are forgotten and they are taken as an end in themselves and as the target of love or when their target is cut off from the figure of Christ or from the mission of the religious.
- Where self-surrender is merely lived for the sake of renunciation, losing sight of its greater aim.

- Where renunciation is accompanied by devaluation and suppression and the value of that which is omitted is denied or impaired.
- Where the God-given life forces remain barren, paralyzed and are no longer available for letting the Kingdom of God in this world take root.
- Where the evangelical counsels are only seen in a legal perspective and therefore curtailing the freedom won by them.[53]

If the witness of religious life remains clear and unambiguous as a way of following Christ and as the free response of love, then these ambiguities would be overcome.

The too much emphasis on the three 'counsels' has impoverished the theology of the religious life, by laying over-emphasis on three qualities to the call of God and ignoring the principal Gospel demands, such as love of enemies and concern for the disadvantaged or the sinned-against and, in many cases, not really touching on the day-to-day experiences of religious life. After all, the virtues that a person is called to exercise, demand a specificity arising from a concrete social situation. The evangelical counsels can be so understood and employed that they favour legalism insofar as they stress the ascetic aspects of individual perfection and minimize the fundamental evangelical renunciation of self in order to centre one's life on the person of Christ and his love for the needy of this world.

Moreover, the doctrine concerning the counsels puts its accent on the precise obligations of the vows and consequently on the sins that one commits in failing to keep these obligations, forgetting that people are not only wilful violators of God's law, or in this case the Church's law, but they are also the violated. This realization must have a bearing on our theology, in our preaching and in our day-to-day interactions. The human person is both an object and at the same time a subject of sin.

Moreover, the lopsided teaching of the triad freezes the theology of the religious life and makes of it a definite state of perfection. It ignores the dynamism of love and the need for creativity and openness to the further demands of the Spirit. The religious life, far from being a fixed entity, is essentially a charismatic gift that impels people into new and unexplored lands.[54] Little wonder many new emerging religious Congregations are adding more and more to the 'conventional' triad; some have up to five vows. The vocation and mission of a religious cannot be confined to a specific activity or apostolate nor can it be defined only in terms of the three so-called evangelical vows. Religious life must be able to manifest in a given situation the different aspects of Christ. In our places of work, in our homes and different communities, there are thousands of opportunities calling us to manifest different aspects of Christ; one time you may be called to show his love and compassion, at another time his patience, kindness, goodness, fortitude and so on. So, bringing Christ to people in different ways, circumstances, in different forms, as the case may be, is also one of the essential elements in the religious vocation and mission.

By way of conclusion, it becomes clear that the mere taking of vows does not give a different or special meaning to our lives. What the vows do is that they make public and explicit our rejection of the values of the society. Obedience, for example, is a clear rejection of the image of the self as autonomous, solitary and disengaged. It is a declaration of our intention to discover who we are in the common life of the brethren. It is a commitment to be liberated from the unsustainable burden of the modern and lonely self. In obedience, we also reject the image of life as the struggle to be strong and in poverty we publicly renounce the competitive struggle for success, the rat race of the consumerist society. In chastity we accept that the deepest fertility and fecundity we can ever be gifted with is that of the creative God who raises the dead.

In order to understand and mature in this religious lifestyle and in living out these vows authentically and fruitfully a novice goes through years of religious formation. The first stage in this formation is a preparation for the taking of the vows. The formation process is that of becoming more and more like Christ, growing in union with Him, taking on His mind and sharing in His sacrifice. It is a process of conversion leading to the perfection of which we mentioned above; *striving continuously to do God's will.* This is a lifelong journey where we seek always to cultivate perseverance and fidelity, hence it is part of the process of living out our life of consecration.

Notes

1 Cf. David FLEMING, 'Understanding a Theology of Religious Life', in: *Religious Life, Rebirth through Conversion*, G. ARBUCKLE & D. FLEMING (eds.), Middle green, Slough 1990, pp. 21-79, here p. 23.

2 Sandra SCHNEIDER, 'Evangelical Equality. Religious consecration, Mission and Witness', in: *Spirituality Today* 39/1 1987.

3 Read Barbara FIAND, Living the Vision, Religious Vows in an Age of Change, New York 1990, pp. 40-44.

4 N. LOHKAMP, 'Consecration, Personal', in: *The New Catholic Encyclopaedia,* Second Edition 4, Thomas Gale, Washington, D.C., 2003, p. 156.

5 The 'world' in question here is the Greek word *cosmos*. *Cosmos* most often refers to the inhabited earth and the people who live on the earth, ungodly multitude, the whole mass of men alienated from God and therefore hostile to the cause of Christ. Satan is the ruler of this '*cosmos'* (John 12:31; 16:11; 1 John 5:19). By the simple definition that the word 'world' here refers to a world system ruled by Satan, we can more readily understand Christ's claims that believers are no longer of the world. That is to say that they are no longer ruled by sin, nor are they bound by the principles of the world. In addition, they are being changed into the image of Christ, causing their interest in the things of the world to become less and less as they mature in Christ.

6 The Holy Scriptures are full of equivocal use of the word 'world'. In many passages 'the world' is the earth, the dwelling place of mankind (Mark 14.9; John 12.25; 16.21; 1 Corinthians 5.10; 1 Tm 6.7), in contrast to heaven, the dwelling place of God, from where Christ came (John 1.9; 3.17; 6.14; 10.36; 13.1; 1 Tm 1.15; 3.16; Hebrews 10.5). The things of 'this

world' are often contrasted with those of heaven (Matthew 16.26; Mark 8.36; Luke 9.25; 1 Corinthians 7.31, 33), and what are earthly or worldly realities with heavenly or spiritual ones (Matthew 16.26; Mark 8.36; Luke 9.25; John 3.31; 1 Corinthians 7.31, 33; Hebrews 8.5; 9.1, 23; 1 John 2.15; 3.17; Ti 2.12). Sometimes 'the world' means mankind itself (Matthew 5.14; 18.7; John 1.29; 3.17; Romans 3.6, 19; 1 Corinthians 1.27), especially those who are the objects of God's love (John 3.16; 6.33, 51; 12.47). In the Johannine writings, 'the world,' i.e., 'mankind,' is indeed generally presented as the object of Christ's saving mission rather than as opposed to His Kingdom; God loves it (John 3.16) and sent His Son to save it (John 3.17); Christ is the light who has come into the world (John 3.19) as its Saviour (John 4.42). By His redemptive sacrifice, Christ has resumed Lordship of 'the world' (Philippians 2.10; John 12.32) and restored the whole cosmos to unity under Himself. God's purpose is 'to re-establish all things in Christ' (Ephesians 1.10). The Church, which is the body of Christ in the new and definitive world order inaugurated by the risen Lord, continues His work in this present 'world' (Colossians 1.18; 3.1–4; Ephesians 1.20–21; John 16.33; 17.20–23). For a more understanding of the varying conceptions of the word 'world' in the Bible read J.L.RONAN, 'World', in: *The New Catholic Encyclopaedia,* Second Edition 14, Thomas Gale, Washington, D.C., 2003, pp. 839-840.

7 Louis E. LOTZ, 'Perplexing text Matthew 5:48', in: *The Reformed Journal*, 29 No 4 1979, p. 8.

8 The stress on the answer given by Dane is just to bring out the core of the dialogue and it is done by me.

9 The word *Apophthegmata Patrum,* literally means 'sayings of the Fathers'. It is the name given to various collections popularly known as the sayings of the Desert Fathers, consisting of spiritual and wisdom stories and sayings attributed to the Desert Fathers and Desert Mothers, from approximately the 5th century AD.

10 Read Thurston Bonnie BOWMANN, 'Expository Articles Matthew 5:43-48', in: *Interpretation* 41 no 2 1987, p.170-173.

11 'And the Two Become One', in: *L'osservatore Romano*, English Weekly Edition, Friday 4th April 2014, pp. 1&3. The full text reads thus: '... The Church is the bride of Christ. This is their relationship. This means that Matrimony responds to a specific vocation and must be considered as a consecration (cf. *Gaudium et Spes*, n.48; *Familiaris Consortio*, n.56). It is a consecration: the man

and woman are consecrated in their love. The spouses, in fact, in virtue of the Sacrament, are invested with a true and proper mission, so that starting with the simple ordinary things of life they may make visible the love with which Christ loves His Church, by continuing to give his life for her in fidelity and service. …'

12 It might be expedient at this point to add that the '*conversatione morum'* (RB 58:17) which is the Benedictine monastic vow par excellence has been taken to be 'monastic life-style', or conversion of manners and the thorough change of the person on a deeper level.

13 George GUIVER, Pursuing the Mystery. Worship and daily life as Presence of God, SPCK London 1996, p. 23.

14 Andreas KNAPP, Brennender als Feuer, Geistliche Gedichte. Mit einem Essay von Bischof Manfred Scheuer, echter Verlag GmbH 2004, p. 20. The English translation is mine.

15 Anneliese HERZIG, 'Lebenskultur nach den evangelischen Räten Antwort – Symbol – Gestaltungsprinzip', in: *Gottes Freundschaft. Ordensleben heute denken*, p. 82.

16 See Anneliese HERZIG, 'Lebenskultur nach den evangelischen Räten Antwort – Symbol – Gestaltungsprinzip', p. 83.

17 In one of his Angelus messages in January, Pope Francis asked for 'a change of attitude on the part of every one, moving away from the attitude of defensiveness and fear, indifference and marginalisation towards attitudes based on a culture of encounter, the only culture capable of building a better, more just and fraternal world'. (Tablet 22 February 2014, p. 16).

18 Karl RAHNER, The Practice of Faith, New York 1983, p. 63.

19 A culture implies the cohesion and consistency of all the elements of life. Such a culture is always and par excellence, the fruit of the experience of a collectivity. In this vein, the vows are religious culture of life par excellence and not a legalistic code of moral do's and don'ts.

20 Read Viktor DAMMERTZ, 'Poverty in the Rule of St Benedict and today', in: *The American Benedictine Review,* 35 1984, pp.1-16.

21 See Anneliese HERZIG, In der Spur Jesu. Leben nach den Evangelischen Räten, Tyrolia, Innsbruck 2012, p. 38.

22 G. MACKRELL, Thoughts for Religious, Middlegreen, Slough, 1984, p. 24-25.

23 See Frieda HADDAD, 'Orthodox Spirituality, The Monastic Life', in: *Ecumenical Review* 38 No 1, 1986, pp. 64-70, here p. 69.

24 Htpp://www.boston-catholic-journal.com chastity-and-charity-beauty-unveiled.pdf. By a cloistered Poor Clare Colettine Nun. p. 2.

25 A.W. Richard SIPE, 'Celibacy' in: *The Oxford Companion to Christian Thought,* Ed. Adrian Hastings New York: Oxford University Press. 2000, p. 104. The stresses on the italics are mine.

26 See A. W. Richard SIPE, 'Celibacy Today. Mystery, Myth and Miasma', in: *Cross Currents* 58 No 4 2008, pp. 545-562. Here pp. 545-547.

27 See Frieda HADDAD, 'Orthodox Spirituality, The Monastic Life', p. 69.

28 Michael CASEY, 'Consecrated Chastity: Reflections on the Text of Gertrude of Helft', 6.

29 See Michael CASEY, 'Consecrated Chastity: Reflections on the Text of Gertrude of Helft', p. 12.

30 For Sartre, *facticity* was the set of facts relevant or given to the person, for example his physical characteristics, his parents, and his unique position. It represents the contingency of human existence and belongs to being-in-itself. According to Sartre, this finitude of human existence does not determine our freedom or our fundamental project. Instead, it is the basis upon which we make our free choices. An infinite being does not need to exercise choice, and human choice consists precisely in discovering a person's *facticity* and seeking to negate or surpass its limitations.

31 Barbara FIAND, Living the Vision. Religious Vows in an Age of Change, p.82.

32 Barbara FIAND, Living the Vision. Religious Vows in an Age of Change, p.82.

33 A. W. Richard SIPE, 'Celibacy Today. Mystery, Myth and Miasma', p. 545.

34 A. W. Richard SIPE, 'Celibacy Today. Mystery, Myth and Miasma', p. 545.

35 Karl RAHNER, The Practice of Faith, p. 63

36 D. O'MURCHU, Religious Life A Prophetic Vision, Notre Dame Indiana: Ave Maria Press, 1991, p.49.

37 T. W. KRENIK, Formation for Priestly Celibacy: A Resource Book, Washington D.C.: National Catholic educational association, 1999, p. 21. The italics are mine.

38 R. J. GUNZEL, Celibacy: Renewing the Gift, Releasing the Power, Kansas: Sheed and Ward, 1988, p. 32.

39 See A. W. Richard SIPE, 'Celibacy Today. Mystery, Myth and Miasma', p. 547. 'Celibate achievement is accountable and, to a degree, measurable. 'By their fruits you shall know them'. Although celibacy is capable of many faces, its moniker is also capable of wearing many masks. Out of all of its manifest variations, permutations, individualizations, frustrations, failures, or perversions, certain qualities measure its authenticity: service, complete self-honesty, awareness of the oneness of the human condition, and the capacity to love'.

40 Diarmuid O' MURCHU, Religious Life A Prophetic Vision, p. 144.

41 Diarmuid O' MURCHU, Religious Life A Prophetic Vision, p. 145.

42 Read Gerald A. ARBUCKLE and David L. FLEMING, Religious Life: Rebirth Through Conversion, p. 29

43 Judith MERKLE, A Different Touch: A Study of Vows in Religious Life, Collegeville, Minnesota: The Liturgical Press, 1998, p. 203.

44 Judith MERKLE, A Different Touch: A Study of Vows in Religious Life, pp. 202-203.

45 David B. KNIGHT, S.J., Joy and Judgement in Religious Obedience, in: Studies in the Spirituality of the Jesuits, Published by the American Assistancy Seminar on Jesuit Spirituality, especially for American Jesuits working out their aggiornamento in the spirit of Vatican Council, Vol. VI, No. 3, 1974, pp. 131-168, here p. 141.

46 See David B. KNIGHT, S.J., Joy and Judgement in Religious Obedience, p. 142.

47 See David B. KNIGHT, S.J., Joy and Judgement in Religious Obedience, p. 143.

48 Based on Judith MERKLE, Committed by Choice, Collegeville, Minnesota: The Liturgical Press, 1992, p. 84.

49 Congregation for Institute of Consecrated Life and Societies of Apostolic Life, *Fraternal Life in Community* Pasay City, Philippines: Daughters of St Paul Publications, 1996, n. 47.

50 Karl RAHNER, 'Reflections on Obedience a basic Ignatian concept', in: *Cross Currents* 10 No 4 1960. Pp 363-374, here pp. 371-372, here p. 372.

51 Karl RAHNER, 'Reflections on Obedience a basic Ignatian concept', p. 372.

52 Karl RAHNER, 'Reflections on Obedience a basic Ignatian concept', p. 372.

53 The five points above are based on the analysis given by Anneliese HERZIG, 'Lebenskultur nach den evangelischen Räten. Antwort – Symbol – Gestaltungsprinzip", pp. 82-83.

54 Read Michel SAUVAGE, Les fondements évangéliques de la vie religieuse, Lassalianum 16 May 1973, pp. 68-71.

III

RELIGIOUS FORMATION AND TRANSFORMATION

THE CONGREGATION FOR Institute of Consecrated life and Societies of Apostolic life on 2nd February 1990, published the Instruction *Potissimum Institutioni,* also known as Directives on Formation in Religious Institutes. According to this document, the most decisive factor of formation, the most important point of the spiritual dimension, the centre of harmony and unity of life, the focal point of identity, has to be sought and found 'in Christ'. In this way, the Instruction present the frame work of the 'four great fidelities,[1]' placing clearly fidelity to Christ and the Gospel in the first place (PI 18):

- fidelity to Christ and the Gospel

- fidelity to the Church and her mission in the world,
- fidelity to the Religious Life and the *Charism* of the Institute
- fidelity to the human person and to our age.

Potissimum Institutioni and *Pastores Dabo Vobis (*1992) both quite rightly stress the need for a comprehensive approach to formation paying attention to providing a solid human formation. We know that it is necessary to incorporate all the dimensions of life in order to become authentic witnesses of God's love. Religious formation should then be a proper preparation of the new candidates to the religious life to live out these 'four great fidelities'.

1. Religious Formation

This chapter considers some foundational aspects of religious formations today, and attempts to understand the purpose and goals of religious formation for individuals and the communities they enter.

In considering the purpose of religious formation it is important to know what formation is: etymologically, the word 'formation' is derived from the Latin verb *formare,* which means 'to mould'. In pedagogy, there are three words that are sometimes confused with 'formation', although they have a similar meaning and signification. These words are 'education', 'instruction' and 'learning'.[2] While 'education' touches the entire person in his/her process of socialization, 'instruction' is the educative act on the part of the educator who aims at transmitting a content of knowledge, and 'learning' is the act on the part of the one who is educated in response to what is being offered in the act of education. The term 'formation' goes beyond these three concepts and its scope is much wider with regards to the formator and the one in formation. Moreover, the generally recognized difficulty of giving a concise definition of formation makes one think that Roger Bulducelli was right when he said: 'Either everyone knows what formation is but no one is telling, or no one is telling because no one knows.'[3] One thing is however clear: religious formation is essentially a growth process which is arrived at through the gradual acquisition of strengths after a successful overcoming of crises, admittance of and learning from failures. Thus formation can be seen as a human process that is capable of leading to personal maturation and the acquisition of personal strengths,[4] comparable to growing from youth to adulthood. Roger Balducelli singles out three crises that a candidate for formation needs to pass through and resolve favourably. 'The first of these is the crisis of intimacy, to be resolved through the decision for celibacy; the second is the crisis of responsibility, to be resolved by a decision for community; the third is the crisis of integrity that comes to resolution in a permanent commitment.'[5]

The continuing progression in formation also implies the restoration of the image and likeness of

God in us which is tainted by sin. This is true of Christian life in general but more so for the religious who is called to live the Christian life in a radical way. Having been stained by sin, we seek through the formation and reformation of our lives a gradual transformation into the original image of God in us. Formation thus becomes a continuous learning process in which one progressively advances to better serve God.

The purpose of formation is thus to accompany the candidate in this arduous process towards Christian maturity thereby leading to the acquisition of a 'particular cultural religious identity'. The constituting elements of this culture are the Scriptures, the particular Constitution of the Religious Congregation, its customs and all its written and oral regulations. All this 'legislation' is not a simple 'law' but the objective expression of the proper identity of a congregation and it is this proper identity that the candidate allows him/herself to be formed in. So through religious formation and the integration of him/herself into the community and the assumption of the particular vision of that community, a candidate gradually develops a personal religious identity. The sign of true religious vocation is manifested in the capacity of a candidate to assume the collective identity while becoming him/herself and develop him/herself in it.

2. *Formation of the Formator*

In talking about formation, the priority of all priorities should be the formation of the formator or formators themselves. This seems to be the most neglected aspect of the formation programme. It is not enough to say that 'we have to look for "good souls"' as formators; this is only an illusion, a good preparation is necessary, indeed indispensable. Otherwise, the formation process would be left to the mercy of the formator's mood swings, likes and dislikes. Ability to accompany others in this arduous journey of becoming whole and holy requires that the formator be in contact with his/her own spiritual development with the ability to foster the process of growth of others.

If we generally believe that competent people should be placed in the most important posts of a congregation, this should also be applied to formation. Suitable and competent religious should be formators, otherwise, long-term objectives are sacrificed to short-term urgent situations, thereby creating a situation of mediocrity in the formation process. In order to ensure that formation is a transforming experience, formators have to be trained to facilitate this process in those receiving it. The Benedictine rule is precise in this regard, for it says that the formator must be one 'who is *skilled* in winning souls', emphasizing this it says: 'one who will *diligently* pay attention to them [novices] in everything' (RB 58:6). So one does not just become a formator, the person needs to posses the necessary skill, competence and suitability. We are not just looking for good souls here, power of transmission is also necessary.

3. Initial Formation

St John Paul II's post-synodol apostolic exhortation, *Vita Consecrata*, 65, says of initial formation:

> The *primary objective* of the formation process is to prepare people for the total consecration of themselves to God in the following of Christ, at the service of the Church's mission. … Since the very purpose of consecrated life is conformity to the Lord Jesus in his *total self-giving*, this must also be the principal objective of formation.

This *total self-giving* means that the initial formation of a religious must include a wide range of elements, namely: *human, spiritual, religious, communal, intellectual* and *apostolic formation*.

Human Formation: (PDV 43)[6] The candidates are formed in cultivating a personal and emotional maturity and developing human qualities necessary for a balanced human and affective development of celibate living and loving. Such qualities will help the candidates to be human and humane.

Spiritual Formation: The candidates are helped and

directed towards having a personal and intimate relationship with God the Father in Jesus Christ. They have to be grounded and appropriate for themselves the Catholic tradition and nurture such a relationship by good habits of prayer, *Lectio Divina* (spiritual reading, especially the reading of the Bible), the sacraments and by self-discipline.

Religious Formation: A formation in acquiring religious identity or religious culture of life. Candidates for religious life are to be moulded to order their lives in accordance with the demands of canon law of the Religious, documents of the Church's magisterium on consecrated life, the Constitutions and customs of their religious institutes.

Communal Formation: Community living in itself is not an easy type of life, also because religious life is simultaneously a life of solitude (in the sense of being a personal encounter with God – me and my God) and a communal fraternal life (this experience of personal relationship with God is lived out among the brethren). These two moments which are paradoxically related to one another should be integrated and balanced for a healthy and supernatural life together. This is an art which needs to be cultivated.

Intellectual Formation: They are to be formed into having a deepened understanding of the mysteries of faith. This will in turn help them to have a spiritual conviction based on faith and not allowing themselves to be shattered with wishy-washy doctrines.

Apostolic Formation: The preceding programmes of formation will prepare the candidates for entering into communion with the charity of Christ (PDV 57). The candidates in apostolic formation learn how to bring the fruit of their lives in compassionate service to the suffering humanity, no matter what their apostolate/ministries are.

To omit or neglect any one of the above elements is to end up with an unbalanced religious.

Moreover, it is indeed necessary to say at the very beginning of religious formation that the aim of formation is not to obtain the transformation of the candidate. Experience has shown us that formation does not necessarily bring about transformation, otherwise the convents and monasteries would be full of angels and saints. Instead the basic reason for religious formation could be seen in the wisdom of St Benedict who in Chapter 58:7 of his Rule for monks made it clear that novitiate formation is a time and a place to find out whether the candidate is 'seeking God'. That is the only condition for admission to profession. 'The concern must be whether the novice truly seeks God and whether he shows eagerness for the Work of God, for obedience and trials.' Besides, religious formation has as its scope the direction of the candidate regarding the rules and regulations of living in a specific congregation. It is also a period to identify the persons that are not yielding to this type of life and withdraw them in time.

Every religious congregation has its own guidelines for those in formation, and it goes beyond the scope of this work to consider these in detail. Instead, I would like to look at several aspects which, in my experience seem to be sorely lacking in formation programmes.

Formation of a 'Sense of Self'

Part of what makes us human beings is that we recognize our own non-necessity,[7] our finiteness. We recognize that we might not be. Death is the paradigm, the evidence of this; human beings live anticipating death. We know that our existence, the fact that we are, is not a necessity. But we also know that who we are is also not necessary. Different decisions and circumstances dramatically affect who we become over the course of a lifetime and each new day opens the possibility that we could become different any time. St Paul is aware of this fact when he says in 1 Corinthians 10:12: 'Therefore let anyone who thinks that he stands take heed lest he fall.' The result of this is a fundamental feeling of insecurity.

The self is a very fragile thing. It is threatened on all sides. How is it to be established and secured? How can we know for sure that we are something good and valuable and worthy of being around, in spite of the fact of our physical and personal non-necessity? We can know that we are, only if we notice others and are noticed by them. If no one notices that we are around, or if we do not notice anybody around us, our lives and our very selves, are in jeopardy. The famous philosophical proposition of René Descartes *cogito ergo sum,* 'I think, therefore I am' meaning that thinking about one's existence proves in and of itself that the person doing the thinking exists. Similarly, the so-called African ethics of *cognatus ergo sum*, 'I am related or I am connected, therefore I am'[8] is a common fact in building a sense of self. Mutually being aware of one another's *Dasein* is self-reassuring. This universal truth is felt more keenly in a celibate vocation. The candidate who is starting his/her faith journey in a religious community requires help and training from the onset so as to develop this sense of self. This is one of the paramount duties of the novice master/mistress. It is in being noticed by others that children come to know that they exist in the first place. If children are noticed, if their presence is acknowledged by others, they gain security and develop a unique sense of self. Moreover, through interactions with other people who affirm or scold them depending on how they behave, children learn what they should and should not do and the traits they should and should not develop. It is similar with novices who are under formation; they need to be acknowledged and guided in whatever they are doing for them to develop a 'sense of self' as a religious, which will lead to a sense of belonging to a given community. The need to be established and sustained in a given religious community can only be met by the development of an awareness that one is profoundly and sincerely appreciated by another or that one feels really accepted and cared for. Because the Novitiate is such a critical time of growth, it is important that the novices receive understanding, acceptance and encouragement from the formator. The formator can achieve this not only by means of individual encounters but also through religious education, both of which in turn help the novice to be able to construct a broader context in which to locate his/her personal experiences and to have some objective means of checking judgments and opinions. The superiors should see to it that the formators are given the means to acquire the knowledge and the skills needed for the guidance and direction of souls.

Lack of 'a Sense of Self'

It is important to put on record here what happens when a healthy sense of self is not encouraged. For some, this deprivation of attention manifests itself in anti-social behavior and a lack of self-worth. For others it results in a desire to draw attention to themselves. It can lead to an attempt at manipulating others, an unhealthy desire for power at other people's expense, backbiting, and other social evils, all in an attempt to 'be somebody'. Sometimes it takes a form which externally appears holy, such as starting a big project or even starting a religious congregation. However, when the intention is not self-less but, indeed, an attempt to get noticed and 'be somebody', the dangers even in such admirable projects turn out to be enormous. Unfortunately, some religious can make enormous sacrifices, which, however, are made with the primary motive of drawing attention and being somebody. I would say, in fact, that every personal and social evil has its root in our need to manipulate the world into paying attention to us. And when the world does not respond – because it, too, is engaged in its own self-securing – our attempts to make it respond become continuously more desperate.

This dynamic is at the root of the achievement-oriented lifestyle and all other self-destructive patterns of social existence. And when our desperate attempts to make the community take notice do not work, we increasingly look for ways to anaesthetize ourselves against the knowledge that we are not being noticed in the way we want or need to be. We can do this through prejudice, vainglory, criticism of the system in the community, criticism of those at the head, or those who we believe are noticed or *in extremis,* we can go to the extent of looking for a way to eliminate them, fabricate lies against them and so on. The other side of deadening oneself to this reality of not being noticed is to fall into deep melancholy, always complaining that nothing is good in this congregation, nothing is working well and that nobody is living the life. In short, everything is going wrong. Here we have a very sad and fastidious religious. This dynamic operates in all of us to one degree or another. That is why it is necessary to dedicate time in the novitiate equipping candidates to deal with this challenge and for all members in the community to remain aware of the need to acknowledge, support and encourage one another.

Formation of Trust

Martin Buber wrote:

> The decisive thing is whether the young people are ready to talk. If someone treats them with trust, shows them that he believes in them, they will talk to him. The first necessity is that the teacher must arouse in his pupils that most valuable thing of all – genuine trust.[9]

The formator should try his/her best to inspire trust. Unfortunately many religious houses today are suspicious of candidates under the pretence of modern psychological assessments. The problem with suspicion is that it predisposes the mind to search for faults in the candidate rather than to hear and see the little grain of truth that he/she is struggling to share, and it certainly does nothing to awaken trust on the side of the suspected candidate. I am not in any way trying to water down the importance of psychological assessments which are necessary in the early years of formation. However, they should be done with love and must not give the impression that we are hunting for errors and scanning for inadequacies and so on. A good psychologist knows that it is his or her job not only to bring the bad to the fore but also the good. In religious life, this truthful acceptance of all qualities in me as they are and in the balance that they exist goes by the name of humility. This humility, this recognition and acceptance of who we are in all our variety, is necessary for future growth. Novices need to be helped to affirm their past experience as relevant and necessary to their mission as it develops through their religious life. They have to learn to accept themselves, and their experiences, as the preparation for the call. After all, as Dolores Hart puts it:

> The doorway that opens to full realization is not a psychological doorway, but it is at the deepest level of our personhood where we are receptive to the love that is always seeking us, bound in union with our love of God and God's love for us. It's when we begin to understand this mystery that we are capable of apprehending ourselves as a new person, able to act in ways that were beyond our own expectations.[10]

So the first task of a formator or formators is to build

up trust and confidence; to give the novices reasons to trust them so that they can feel safe to be their real selves. They ought not to feel that they are continually being scrutinized; otherwise they will end up worrying, saying to themselves 'that if the brethren were to see what we are really like, then they might not vote for us for profession.'[11] The temptation would be to conceal who they are until they are safely and securely inside, professed and ordained and invulnerable. To accept this would be to settle for a formation in deceit, said Fr Radcliffe. The novices should also be encouraged to trust themselves, for 'it is usually those in formation who form each other most.'[12] The religious life is not meant for loners, but for those who have confidence in each other's strengths.

Formation in Compassion

Another word for compassion is mercy or *misericordia* in Latin. St Augustine points out that mercy 'gets its Latin name, *misericordia,* from the sorrow of someone who is miserable; it is made up of two words, *miser,* 'miserable' and *cor,* 'heart'. It means being heartsore. So when someone else's misery or sorrow touches and pierces your heart, it is called *misericordia,* or soreness of heart.'[13] In another place Augustine writes '*Misericordia* is so called because it makes *miserum* the heart, *cor,* of someone who feels compassion for another's misfortune.'[14] So, many Latin writers but most especially Augustine exploit the possibilities of the antithesis *miseria/misericordia.* This is so for Augustine because he was so much aware of his misery and of the mercy God had shown him.

It is worthwhile to stress that compassion is another indispensable area of formation, or as Timothy Radcliffe says, 'an education of the heart and the mind that breaks down everything within us that is stony-hearted, priggish, arrogant and judgmental.'[15] The gift of one's life is the most precious gift that a novice brings to the religious congregation which he/she joins.[16] This valuable gift comes with all its baggage of *miseria,* failures, difficulties, dark moments and in a word with all its *facticity,*[17] but if taught to have compassion, a novice might come to see some of his/her past failures as *felix culpa,* serving and disposing him/her better for compassion, for indeed to have compassion with others requires that we also have compassion with ourselves.

Formation in 'Suspecting the Good'

In the Primitive Constitution of the Dominicans, one of the tasks of the novice master was to teach the novices to 'suspect the good'.[18] This is a wonderful value that needs to be re-evaluated in the formation of novices and professed religious today, because it is the summary and the explanation of what Christian love means. What this implies is that we give the best possible interpretation to what a brother/sister does or says. For example, if a brother/sister comes back regularly late at night, instead of imagining the terrible sins he/she must have committed, you trust, to the extent circumstances allow, that the brother/sister has a valid reason for the tardiness rather than jumping immediately to uncharitable conclusions. In some respects, this should not be difficult: religious share a common patrimony; and therefore the reputation of one affects that of the other. If it proves necessary to call the person's attention to the fault, this too must be done in all charity and purity of mind, a disposition which can easily be assessed when one critically examines the reasons for confronting the other person. If one can confront the other without judgment, and without presuming that one knows what he/she has been doing and therefore why he/she comes regularly late, one not only guards one's soul from falling into sins potentially far more dangerous than those that one is trying to correct but also raises the chances of being met by someone prepared to listen to what one has to say.

This is a quality which only mature people have and helping religious to develop this quality, and to mature more generally, is an important part of religious formation. Maturity takes many different forms. If there is anything one learns in a community it is that people mature differently. Some may be intellectually mature but spiritually immature, some may be socially mature amongst their peers but don't know how to live with people outside their comfort zone. However, there are two definite signs of immaturity which pose specific challenges to religious life: when people are centered on themselves and when they cannot accept or cope with the essential imperfections of life in our world, in our Church and in our religious communities. For such people the problems are always outside themselves. Everything would be fine if only the situation in which they found themselves was different, if Brother/Sister or Father X was not in the community, if there was a different superior, if their work was different or if they didn't have to work with this or that person. Mature people, on the other hand, accept imperfect situations and make the best of them, and they think of others and put others before themselves. Savonarola wrote a letter centuries ago to a novice who had been scandalized by the sins of the brethren. He warned him about people who join the Order hoping to enter paradise right away. They never last, he said. 'They wish to live among the saints, excluding all wicked and imperfect people. And when they do not find this, they abandon their vocation and take on the road … But if you wish to flee from all the wicked, then you must leave this world,'[19] because the world, which the religious is part of, is full of wickedness. This confrontation with human fragility is a wonderful moment in the maturing of a vocation and a sign of human maturity too. One learns to make the best of very imperfect and difficult situations, and is trained by it to cope and become mature in the process. Training the religious to suspect the good is a way of helping them become more flexible and open to other positions. It helps the religious to become capable of adapting him/herself and his/her opinions, without losing his/her center. 'Suspecting the good' helps the religious to cope with the conflicts inherent in human existence and learn how to cope with the tensions inherent in community living and notwithstanding have a genuine peace of heart. With certainty this is not something which anyone perfects in the novitiate; it is an element of ongoing formation which is vital for all religious and which helps them to grow in love and compassion for all.

Formation for Community Living

The widely acknowledged problem today regarding community living is because it has long been taken for granted. As novices leave initial formation and enter programmes of advanced study or take up individual ministries in professional settings, they may find themselves living in mixed groups or singly and in some cases they might also be living in colleges with other lay students. This being the situation it is necessary that formation for community be incorporated in formation programmes so that the novices become interiorly formed for community life in all its theological, spiritual, ministerial and affective concreteness.[20] In this formation programme for community living novices are to be helped in some essential dimensions aligned to community living. Such as in:

Affective Formation: Since they freely joined this community of their 'choice', they have to learn to love their community. Unless one belongs affectively to a community, no amount of forced togetherness would get one into community. This affective belonging would be acquired by means of study of the community history, the celebration of community's feast, caring for and recreating with the older members so as to learn from them, learning about the apostolate of the older members by visiting them, taking great pride in the community's achievements and sharing faith. People love by being loved; by getting to know those who love them; by having the chance to express their love and having those expressions recognized and treasured.

Religious and Theological Formation: Community has to be the object of serious study and the subject of profound prayer so that it can be interiorized as a principal value of religious life for which one is prepared to make a real sacrifice over the course of one's life (time).

Spiritual-ascetical Formation: This implies learning the *charism* and the culture of a given community. There is nothing like belonging to a community 'in general'. We belong to 'a particular community'. The spirit or the *charism* of a given community is not taught in a classroom but it has to be caught, sensed, and breathed-in through actual participation in community life. The *charism* of a given community being Scripture abridged gives life, sense, character, form and personality to the community. So the novices have to discover and learn this experientially and interiorize this spirit.

Asceticism: Community life is not easy and living it requires its own asceticism and this asceticism must be acquired in formation.

Commitment to giving priority attention to community affairs: this is also a form of asceticism that is almost impossible to any professed member if it has not been learnt and practised in the initial formative years.

Community life is integral to Christian and religious existence and therefore should be interiorly cultivated by one who is aspiring to be part of a religious family. The novice master/mistress and the entire community are all responsible for the formation of the new members, especially in this regard.

Formation in Theological Education

When we speak of the formation of religious what generally comes to mind is the spiritual and theological formation proper to vocation, not the technical and professional formation of skills that are traditionally the realm of laypeople. Unfortunately, this is not the case in many congregations. If one examines the programme of formation of many religious congregations, what one sees is that women religious are first generally trained in their own houses and mainly for the service of their own communities: for the kitchen, for the laundry, for the garden, etc. Then there is training for works done outside the enclosure, mainly teaching and nursing, but always with a training given inside, in their own institutes and for their own institutions. After their first profession some religious go on to study in secular colleges and universities. Such training is certainly important but my concern is that the basic theological training necessary for embracing the vowed life is given far too little room. One can rightly point out that religious men who are trained for the priesthood necessarily receive a solid basis in theology. Apart from them, though, only those few who are privileged to do some theological courses after their profession are intellectually equipped to grapple with this necessary aspect of religious life. As it is central to the religious life of each individual, basic theological education such as Catholic dogma, Church history, Old and New Testament, theology of the vows, the Rule/Constitution and the *Charism* of the Congregation ought to be required for all.[21] Even when it might seem secondary to the work being done by a particular congregation, we must understand that this is in fact the one thing which is absolutely necessary for a job to become a true apostolate and for a person to grow as a Christian. Of course, not everyone has the same needs or intellectual capacities. Some people will profit from more intensive studies whereas others will find a more basic approach sufficient. In some cases a cycle of well-organized courses is called for, in others the tutorial system might be judged more suitable. Such matters are secondary and must be determined on a case-by-case basis. However, the need for a theological basis must be seen as universal for healthy religious vocations and not as something reserved for a few sisters or for brothers training for the priesthood. The importance of such theological knowledge was evident in the Instruction *Renovationis Causam,* which stressed the need of using the broad principles of the *conciliar Magisterium* to shed light on the matter of formation. The Instruction recalled, for example, 'that the basic task of formators was to bring candidates gradually to a full identification with the Christ of the Gospel, and that their main concern should be to help them take upon themselves, with an ever greater sense of responsibility, both the positive and the renunciatory aspects characteristic of the following of Christ as proposed in the Gospel.'[22] The Document says: 'In the direction of the novices, particularly during the periods of formative activity, the Novice Master [Mistress] will base his [her] direction on the teaching so clearly enunciated by the Second Vatican Council: 'Therefore, in order that members may above all respond to their vocation of following Christ and may serve Christ Himself in His members, their apostolic activity should result from their intimate union with Him' [PC 8]" (RC 31).

We are all aware that the social and economic changes of our time are forcing religious to look for technical and professional formation and the thrust of the Church initiated by the *Second Vatican Council* and the corresponding renewal of Religious Life has stressed a people-centered vocation of the Church, thereby emphasizing the need for religious to be involved in the life of the world and particularly the world of the workers (cf. PC 13 and ET 20). The Document issued by the Sacred Congregation for Religious and Secular Institutes in 1981 is explicit on this point, saying:

> Faced with such a vast sector of humanity, which strongly challenges the mission of the entire Christian Community, religious feel a deeper need for solidarity and sharing. They feel that their choice of evangelical poverty itself places on them the obligation to accept the authentic values of the common law of work.[23]

Certainly, we know that the need for involvement in work in the world and for qualified personnel is in itself a sort of commitment towards a more realistic and incarnated way of living the vow of evangelical poverty in solidarity with all those millions of people who depend on their daily work for their own subsistence. It is to take seriously the spirituality lived by Jesus Himself during the long years of his life in Nazareth where He was known not only as the 'son of the carpenter' but as 'the carpenter', (cf. Mark 6:3; Matthew 13:55). Even so, such a technical formation will not have any 'moral' or 'spiritual' dimension for the religious if he/she is not well rooted in the teachings of the Church and immersed in the religious cultural lifestyle of the promises which he/she made. Without this theological basis, he/she is just like any other layperson at work. Little wonder then some religious do not know how to do their technical jobs as 'religious brothers and sisters'. So before and above all these technical formations, novitiate formation should be, if possible, solely or pre-eminently geared towards the theological formation of candidates. The importance and necessity for such theological formation cannot be overemphasized, for the reason that the inordinate thirst for 'apparitions', 'visions' and extraordinary happenings, which one finds in many congregations, and among so many religious men/women, often comes from an insufficient knowledge of the essential Christian message and also from lack of faith.

Up to this point the stress has been on initial formation. And it is true, the introduction into such theological education is done in the novitiate; however the rest is studied throughout life. The novitiate is the place to develop a religious identity and a deeper spirituality. It is a period in which novices set down roots in the soil which will nourish their vocation for the rest of their lives. For this reason it is such a critical period. Only when this has been done can they move forward in their ongoing formation, deepening their theological knowledge as they learn more both intellectually and in the practical Christian life and assimilate this Christian message into their own lives. The theological education in question here should not be just an academic discipline but rather should aim at opening the novices' minds to the breadth and height and depth of the love of God. The study of theology and scripture is not going to be an add-on or a mere addendum like learning to sew or to cook as all other technical training, rather it is taught in such a way that it achieves its aim: growth in love of God and neighbour, for 'knowledge precedes love'. We study in order to understand, in order to be reformed, in order to serve, and ultimately in order to love. Our study is meant to overflow into praise, worship, happiness and make us truly compassionate human beings. Therefore, the success of initial formation can be measured not so much by how much knowledge one has acquired, but by the fact that a brother/sister has been 'formed in the freedom to learn throughout life, in every age and season, in every human ambient and context, from every person and every culture open to be taught by any fragment of truth and beauty found around them', and has learnt 'to be formed by everyday life, by their own community, by their brothers and sisters, by everyday things, ordinary and extraordinary, by prayer and by apostolic fatigue, in joy and in suffering, until the moment of death.'[24]

Formative Power of the Religious Community (Congregation)

The modality in which each concrete community (Congregation) lives out the spirit of communion *koinonia,* has a very profound influence on the human, psychological and spiritual development of novices. In addition to formation proper, which it offers to its members, the religious community as such has formative power in the lives of novices and this role is of utmost importance. It can nurture their faith and give shape to the quality and character of their spirits. Faith is formed, developed, and owned in the context of communities; this cannot be left to the Master/Mistress of novices alone. Spirituality deepens in community rather than in individualistic isolation. The beliefs, values, attitudes, stories, rituals, and moral practices of one's religious community are the human forces most powerful in shaping a person's spiritual journey. Moreover, there are so many socializing and enculturating forces working in people's lives in our contemporary, highly mobile, technological and pluralistic culture that the formative power of religious communities, especially on congregational levels seems rather weak in comparison. Furthermore, as we all can testify with experience, congregations are not always all that faithful. More often than not, and in many ways, they seem more a reflection of the wider culture's values (and, too often, some of its worst) than something that is really 'radical' or 'counter-cultural', which they are supposed to be. These are extremely difficult problems in counting or totally depending on the faith and spirit forming powers of religious communities.

A basic reality of life in many religious congregations today is that they are engaged in socially acceptable (indeed, socially celebrated) patterns of mutual self-destruction.[25] This particular pattern is called by social psychologists 'the achievement-oriented lifestyle'. The achievement-oriented lifestyle is a style of life which has as its centre the *compulsion* to succeed or to achieve in whatever social world one lives. A person whose lifestyle is grounded on the achievement motive is one whose self-image depends upon 'making it' in one way or another. Who one is, one's identity, depends upon *earning* the affection and recognition of others through the value of what one produces or does. The stress is on doing and not on being; what you do or what you achieve is equated with who you are. This *compulsion* to achieve affects, almost to the point of determining, one's behaviour, attitudes, values, and fundamental beliefs. This is because a lifestyle is, according to James E. Loder, 'centrally a matter of personal, social, and cultural integration based on a formal pattern which pervades and interrelates the registers of behavior, shaping and directing a personality through scores of varied activities and extremities.'[26] That is why a religious brother/sister would introduce him/herself in public first as a medical doctor, a professor of philosophy or theology, a nurse, a midwife, a sister or brother or Rev. Fr Dr, and mention only later, if at all, that they are brothers/sisters/priests. This is a consequence of the social behaviours of the society in which they live; brother/sister feels good by earning the affection and the recognition of the people through his/her degrees. In so doing, we forget the consequence of our calling: to be *counter-cultural.* Achievement motive, when applied to anything apart from Christian virtues, indeed robs us of our religious/priestly identity and makes us less enthusiastic about the things that matter most in our lives as religious/priests. The three evils which conspire together to dampen our zeal for the service to which we are called are: a heightened individualism, a crisis of identity and a cooling of fervour. (See Pope Francis, Apostolic Exhortation on the Proclamation of the Gospel, *Evangelii Gaudium,* 78.)

An example of one who has and was able to affirm and reaffirm his identity with enthusiasm and vigour is the South African anti-apartheid revolutionary and politician who served as President of South Africa from 1994 to 1999 Nelson Mandela. In his autobiography, *The Long Walk to Freedom*, Nelson Mandela describes his great pride and joy when he bought his first house in Johannesburg. It was not much, but he had become a man. A man must own land and beget children. This of course is what gives him identity and status. But because of his struggle for his people, he hardly lived in his house or saw his family. He made a choice which, in effect, proved to be a renunciation of what gives people identity in the world of the global market; the status that comes with income, the ability to be someone who buys and sells and one who is 'someone'. He did so in such a radical way that his actions ought to resonate with those living the religious life. As he reflected:

> It was this desire for the freedom of my people to live their lives with dignity and self respect that animated my life, that transformed a frightened young man into a bold one, that drove a law abiding attorney to become a criminal, that turned a family loving husband into a man without a home, that forced a life living man to live like a monk. I am not more virtuous or self-sacrificing than the next man, but I found that I could not even enjoy the poor and limited freedom I was allowed when I knew my people were not free. Freedom is indivisible; the

> chains on any one of my people were the chains on all of them; the chains on all my people were the chains on me.[27]

If indeed we are 'leaving behind worldly identities', then the formative power of a religious community would be very effective because such a community must have developed a solid local religious culture. Such a culture implies a clear common vision of the religious life and a spiritual orientation which conditions and gives form to all the elements of daily life that is without doubt counter-cultural. In a community/congregation where such a culture exists, the role of the novice masters/mistresses will consist essentially in helping the novices to participate in it and to allow themselves to be formed by it and to make it their own in a responsible and creative way. On the other hand, if it does not exist 'all the "techniques" of formation that may be used (courses, meetings counseling etc.) will in general have very little result.'[28]

Reason Behind this 'Quest for Achievement Motive' and its Negative Effect on Formation of Novices

We are all aware that there is nothing that people need and want more than to be loved and found worthy – just for who they are. There are some who lacked unconditional affection in their early childhood training. Affection sometimes can be used as a manipulative device. It could be withheld until the child performs well; or bestowed with excessive intensity and enthusiasm when the child has done something that makes the parents proud. This same pattern continues, and indeed is intensified, in the school situations. In school, the ones who develop a sense of self-worth are those who produce. They get the grades or other social rewards. They get the affection of their teachers. They get the acclamation of their classmates; and the more people succeed, the more they reap the benefits of the social system. There are rewards for those who achieve. Those who do not achieve have no real place in the social matrix. Moreover, it is because of this tendency that the society considers monastic life as a useless kind of life, because the people there are seen as non-achievers. There is evidence for this in our treatment of the mentally ill, the 'uneducated', the physically blemished, and economically poor people. Furthermore, this whole system of social priorities is socialized by the language patterns, symbols, images, and rituals which in general define our culture. Indeed, the achievement motive is a socially acceptable, even socially celebrated, pattern of social interaction. Who, really, argues with success, especially when that success is earned? But it is a 'pattern of mutual self-destruction', because it offers no room for the unsuccessful and for the misfits. The achievement-oriented society and culture gives birth to persons who do indeed produce and are purposeful. But they also tend to manipulate others for their own purposes and suffer from debilitating internal stress. Why? Because becoming an achiever costs something. One pays the price by repressing the need to be loved unconditionally or one represses others such that the poor pay the price in their stead. That is exactly what is happening today in many countries especially in the so-called Third World. 'The central tendency of achievement-orientation is repressive of a deep human cry for assurance of ascriptive (not achieved) worth. The outcome is aggression, tension, domineering control, and cruelty.'[29] This repression is self-destructive and destructive of others. It is self-destructive, not only because it produces ulcers, but more fundamentally because it locks the door to the one thing on which human life most fundamentally depends: unconditional love.

If taken to its natural and extreme point, the achievement-oriented lifestyle, produces people who are utterly, deeply, existentially convinced that they cannot be loved just as they are with all their failures, inadequacies, and finitude. They are driven to earning love. But earned love is not what gives us life; only unearned love does that, because only unearned love is fully love (cf. Romans 5:8) 'what proves that God loves us is that Christ died for us while we were still sinners.' So, by being compelled to earn love, we forfeit the possibility of receiving what we most truly and basically need. It is mutually destructive, not only because aggression and cruelty (however subtle) tend to maim those towards whom it is directed, but also because those who cannot receive unearned love cannot give it either.

We have here, then, a pattern of socially acceptable mutual self-destruction in our society. What is much worse, is that this pattern pervades the Church and therefore our religious communities. Achievement as a compulsion is fostered, accepted, and even celebrated in the Church as much as anywhere. Sometimes persons who are honoured in churches are persons who are purposeful, productive, and accomplished, persons who excel and achieve in and out of the Church. The same thing is also very true of religious houses. The most destructive part is that these fundamental patterns are institutionalized, passed on from generation to generation, and become the patterns of personality within which individuals are virtually compelled to act, feel, think, and even imagine. To see how this is so, it is helpful to give few practical examples of this disease which is now eating up and thereby touching the real essence of religious life in some of our societies.

In some modern societies, it is almost a criminal offence for a parent to scold their children, criminal too for a teacher to 'correct' a pupil. Consequently this becomes a normal way of life both in and outside religious milieu. Therefore, in some of the religious houses and communities in Europe 'every person is presumed to be mature and is expected to use his/her reasoning faculty'. They know what they need in and from life and they are left to go for it. Nobody ever thinks of helping to call the other person back to reason; everybody is free to act according to conscience, forgetting that conscience is the most elastic thing an individual possess. In communities like this, one begins to wonder what the vow of obedience means and how possible it is for a novice to learn and understand what obedience means, when he/she on entering has become an automatic mature person in the midst of all mature persons. And indeed, in such cases they necessarily have a very different and accommodative interpretation of all the vows.

Another example can be seen in some African countries. It has long been a usage in some tribes in Nigeria, to offer in return gifts to one's guests after any big celebration. The host quite often depicts his/her image or picture on a plate, or T-shirt, cup, trays, saucers and so on and offers such items to their guests after such big ceremonies in appreciation either of what they have brought or for attending the ceremony. Obviously, such a gift normally requires a colossal amount of money. This custom is gradually permeating Nigerian society to the extent that it is followed even among religious brothers/sisters. On any religious profession or priestly ordination and on celebration of jubilees people feel somehow required to do the same thing, and if they have no money some benefactors somewhere would willingly do it for them. The society is almost luring them into spending such amounts of money, something which flagrantly goes against the vow of poverty. If you happen to ask any of them why they allow themselves to do such a thing, the answer will simply be: 'That is the way it is done.'

We forget that we are called by virtue of our religious commitment to call into question the way things are done, when they go against the vows we have taken and the Gospel principles. In such cases can the novice master/mistress convincingly talk of poverty to the novices when what he/she is seeing is far from being poverty? This reveals, I believe, certain important dynamics going on in the daily lives of many people in our culture and in many of our religious houses. The compulsive and pervasive nature of these patterns of mutual self-destruction is what is killing the formative nature of religious communities in our societies today, because critical reflection upon these facts is difficult to attain.

One of the reasons for the inability to offer critical reflection is because they operate largely at a pre-reflective level. As Edward Farley points out in another (but correlative) context, it is 'too close to see because we 'see' by means of it, that is, through a consciousness already modified by it.'[30] Besides, that explains also the importance of withdrawal from the world that Canon 607 § 3 emphasizes 'The public witness to be rendered by religious to Christ and the Church entails a separation from the world proper to the character and purpose of each institute.' This separation from the world does not necessarily mean physical separation but certainly demands separation from the way the world thinks. It is separation from the way things are done in the society and therefore a separation from this pattern of mutual destruction. In a religious congregation where such evil thrives the authentic formation of the novices is an impossibility because with their very eyes they are seeing the model of the life in the professed religious and therefore in congregation/community. The novice master/mistress cannot form them differently from what is evident in the community.

4. *In Constant Search for Faithfulness:* Ongoing Formation

The ongoing formation of religious is understood as a constant personalization and interiorization of Christ's life. Consequently it is a learning process, which involves change, growth, re-formation and transformation of the individual. We are told that from the point of view of Canon Law, 'perpetual profession, [is] the point of arrival, and at the same time it is the point of departure in religious life, integrally and progressively lived in the institute, and calls for the continual deepening of formation by responding to ever new necessities, thus rendering the religious capable of dynamic fidelity to God's design in the ever-changing circumstances and needs of the Church and the world.'[31] It is in this sense that ongoing formation has been considered to begin only after initial formation is completed when the religious, presumably must have been a mature adult and must have possessed a deep motivation and capacity for an enduring renewal.

However, it should be remarked that strictly speaking ongoing formation is an action that has its beginning right from the very start of religious formation, and is composed of different levels of learning each of them having intermediate goals as the individual acquires knowledge, skills, abilities and competencies. Each of these levels makes available the inclusive formation of the individual by creating favourable conditions of time, space, place and providing the necessary input for growth in religious life. Thus, we should consider formation as ongoing, even though in practice it could be broken up in different stages.

Hence, we can have formation in the pre-novitiate period called postulancy, which has its specific goals to help the candidate prepare for the novitiate. The novitiate in its turn provides the specific formation to help the novice prepare for the first religious profession, which is followed by a post-novitiate formation which also has specific goals to help the young religious to put into practice and deepen the principles given in the earlier periods of vocational growth.

Having gone through the learning processes in the initial formation, that is, formation of a sense of self, formation of trust, formation in compassion, formation in suspecting the good, formation in theological education and other areas of formation available to different congregations, at this point a solid root has been set in the soil. Therefore, ongoing formation will only facilitate the continuing growth of the whole person and promote a deeper and fuller commitment to the Person and mission of Christ. It is no longer a period of acquiring more information or knowledge or a time to produce people who are better informed, but it is above all geared at helping the person to believe more in him/herself, to believe more in life, and to believe more in Christ and His Church. This demands a continuing conversion as a person moves forward in growth towards a more complete realization of the fullness of the Person of Christ within oneself.[32]

Ongoing formation cannot be limited to some definite chronological moment when some formative service is provided; nor can it be restricted to some intensive periods in the life of the religious (a spiritual retreat, an updating course, professional training programme, etc.).[33] But, ongoing religious formation is intimately connected with the regular process of growth of the consecrated person and at every moment of his/

her existence. It is an integral growth of the individual who is in a continuous process of maturation.

There are different elements that make up the consecrated person's life (interior life, apostolic life, affective life, interpersonal relationship, intimacy with God, etc.) and, in the process of growth and maturity, each of these elements, and all these elements should likewise grow. Such an integral growth will take place through the continuous assimilation of the evangelical values, of prayer and of the study of the Word of God, and of full participation in the sacraments.

In the maturation and growth of one's consecration there are three points of reference singled out by Sante Bisignano, and each of these three elements is to become evident and visible.

1. The following of Christ is the first and fundamental criterion of consecration; namely, to follow Christ poor, chaste and obedient in day-to-day life situations.
2. The second criterion consists in living out, as best as possible, the Gospel message and the Gospel value to the point of being a valid witness and testimony to the world.
3. The third criterion consists in the commitment to the ecclesial mission through the fulfilment of service to humanity in the world.[34] These three fidelities become reference points of the maturation process of the religious: fidelity to Christ, fidelity to humanity, and fidelity to the Church.

Ongoing Formation Facilitates Self-awareness for the Good of the Community

Going through the different stages of formation and continuing it after final profession is also intended to result in the discovery of a brother's/sister's special authority, what we can call his/her domain. The process of discovering the domain of each individual brother/sister is a corporate effort of the community and not only of the novice masters/mistresses. 'Everyone should somehow get involved as the brother/sister considers his/her genealogy and instinctual depth, or *bona;* his/her essential background of professional excellence, or *dona;* his/her knowledge of self, or *cura.* Spiritual depth and capacity for care of the community are informed by these fields and allow each man/woman to see how he/she can become a leader for the good of the community.'[35] This is also a realization or an awareness that comes during the long process of ongoing formation.

Stages in the Ongoing Search for Faithfulness

Vita Consecrata, 70, mentions several stages along life's journey in the religious' ongoing search for faithfulness to their commitment:

- The *First Years after final profession* are the first years of full involvement in the apostolate marked by the passage from a supervised life to a situation of full responsibility for one's work. Here, there is need for support and accompaniment.

- *Middle Age* presents risk of routine and the temptation of being disappointed with meagre results. Formation here should be geared towards renewal of their original decision by means of the Gospel values and the charism of the Institute. This is the time to search for what is essential.
- *The stage of Maturity* usually brings personal growth and also with it the possible danger of individualism, inflexibility, self-centredness or diminished enthusiasm. This is more so for those with strong temperaments and outstanding competence: this is a time when everything seems to be called into question. Formation geared at bringing back fervour with a fresh spiritual and theological pabulum and for a more meaningful community life.
- *Advanced Age,* poses problems due to a gradual withdrawal from activity, caused by either sickness or forced immobility. There is need for spiritual support in order to utilize the chance of their suffering to be transformed by the Paschal experience and be configured to the Crucified Christ, who abandons himself into the Father's hands.
- *Completion of Formation* at the moment of death. The gradual nature of continuing formation, which is the longer and most fruitful period in

the life of a religious and only comes to an end with death, should stand out more clearly. This is so because religious formation needs to address different stages of human development and help the individual to give meaning to each stage. As in everything else, what it means to believe changes over the years, that is to say, there is no solid state; rather, in the initial formation candidates have one version of faith, in the ongoing formation another, and so on into old age. There is, of course, a certain amount of continuity but inevitably over the years some kind of religious experience come to the fore while others recede.

As we can see the stages singled out by *Vita Consecrata* correspond to the critical points in the growth of the individual, which is made of ups and downs, cross-roads and critical junctures. It would be folly if ongoing formation is blind to this reality and treat this long period the same way. There should be structures that are highly pliable and adaptable to unique personal situations. However, there should be readiness on the part of the religious to be formed. The Document says, '*Initial* formation, then, should be closely connected with *continuing* formation, thereby creating a readiness on everyone's part to let themselves be formed every day of their lives' (VC 69). This readiness of being daily formed also demands openness to change within and outside of the community. Besides, it can be much easier for people to open themselves to change outside their own environment, because within, they often find themselves categorized in a way that makes it very difficult to change. There is a great need, therefore, for reasonably extended sessions in which professed religious can learn anew the ways of the Church and society in an unthreatening atmosphere.

Formation for Advanced Age or 'Third Age'

Once upon a time one elderly sister, who had held various high offices in her religious congregation over the course of her life and was also once a mother general, said to me: 'My calling is to be a servant, like it's been all my life. But it means something different now. At this stage in my life, being a servant means letting go, passing on the responsibility, and being willing to receive from others. After a lifetime of doing for others, I have to learn to let others do for me. It's not easy.' The conversation went into great depth. But then something became evident and clear: in spite of this sister's conviction of her calling to be a servant and her readiness to accept the different shapes that this very call has taken, she did not know how to handle this period of transition. Just as a new candidate who enters religious life is coached to embrace the life and answer his/her call, we all need help when we move from one stage of life to another. At this stage, the religious, instead of being caught up in the toil and moil of office or ministry, ought to leave everything to the Lord to complete and should be content to see the younger ones take over the responsibility without having the fear that they are less capable. But how practically are they going to be coached?

Formation of 'Meaning'

At this advanced stage, the vitality of a person, the truth and graciousness of their lives depend upon supply of meaning. So the ongoing religious formation at this stage could consider a formation of 'meaning' as a major sector to the ageing years of the religious. It is frustrating for a lot of older members who were once active to no longer be able to do what they once did. This is a challenge for them, not least in that it requires them to reconsider their identity as religious. Given this situation, is it not also important that we draw up some relevant programme for them in continuing their formation? Though they have meaning, a purpose for being where they are as they are, but often they require what Ross Snyder calls 'meaning formation'.[36]

Meaning arises out of mutuality, out of an interweaving of relationships. Meaning is sustained in relationship. In some sense we feel our lives to have meaning when we matter to someone else and when someone else matters to us. Of course, the deepest meaning for any religious must be found in communion with Jesus Christ, but this very communion is easier to live when it is also experienced in communion with others. Something with meaning also has a direction. It is the opposite of a 'dead end'. We have to help our advanced members to recognize and come to terms with the fact that even if they are no longer able to do what they used to do, they are still able to do something. They should not be left redundant because they still have a future that is directed towards a total conformity with Christ. 'The elderly are called in many ways to live out their vocation: by persevering prayer, by patient acceptance of their condition, and by their readiness to serve as spiritual directors, confessors or mentors in prayer' (VC 44).

We need to ask what is being done or not being done which affects the individual's sense that there is meaning in life. The religious perspective raises the question of what can be done to sustain and nurture meaning. Meaning here is 'realized meaning', that is self-fulfillment and aiming at a goal, rather than simply intellectualized meaning. In every situation we need to ask what it is that helps our elderly members to feel that life is worth living, to be able to say yes to life and to God and to be willing to die, saying yes to both death and life.

Human beings are 'meaning makers'. To be human is to discover, uncover and recover meaning. This is a lifelong task. It is affected by what goes on at the biological, psychological, and social levels, but is not identical with any of the changes at these levels. So the community could still help their members to re-create or to re-discover meaning if at this stage the person has lost all meaning of life. The indispensable need for a sense of self in the initial formation would help the person at this stage to look for meaning in Christ and in him alone and not in the offices which he/she held that have passed on to the younger generation.

In order to do all these for the elderly members of our communities, we could consider organizing a programme whereupon they have an opportunity of recounting the wonders of their life, the difficult experiences they went through and how they were able to overcome these difficulties. This kind of recounting of different challenges one went through is called by Ross Snyder 'the saga of one's life', for he says: 'Saga is more than reminiscing, more than anecdotes. Deeper than "the story of my life" Saga is "my journey with the wild energies of God". … This saga gives meaning and song, direction and integrity, to my whole life.'[37]

To get to the level of saga is to get at what it is that has given one's life meaning, direction, and integrity. It is to get at the 'song' that one's life has been. What song have I been singing with my life? In order to find this 'song', I must attend to the critical and formative moments. Snyder calls them the 'lived moments' in my life history. I must try to discover what it was that has enabled me to 'come through', to persevere in the midst of difficulties. I must give attention to the points at which there were breakthroughs to new life, highlighting and underlining God's interventions and presence at every stage. These, as they are linked together in one life history, reach the level of what is called the 'Saga of my life'.

It is this linking together that Snyder also calls 'membering', joining the parts into a whole, this is what memory work struggles to do. Through memory and reflection one tries to find what has tied life together and what could tie life together for him/her still. This re-membering, or membering, for Snyder is related to both the past and the present. In it, the religious become aware not only of their past, of people and ideas but also of the Gospel episodes which they have interiorized and which have become part of them and given form to their meanings, values, and purposes, being called to share in Christ's awareness of the Father and in his compassion towards human beings.

The Religious meaning formation at this stage therefore is meant to help the older members of our communities to continually remind themselves of the goal of religious life, which is to be conformed to the Word through the imitation of Christ. It is a question of striving always to put on Christ (Galatians 3:27, Romans 13:14), of striving always to have the mind of Christ (1 Corinthians 2:16, Philippians 2:5), of striving always to enter personally into the Word and let it permeate their being, so that they no longer view things from a merely human standpoint. Through all these, they are able to arrive at a new way of being, open to the voice of God and learning who they really are in Him both individually and corporately.

The Saga of One's Life

Unfortunately, many of the older members in religious communities were never equipped with the skills to articulate their sagas and as they advance in life it is very hard to learn. That is why initial formation is so important. However, in the event that they do have the capacity to articulate, what they need is space to share. What we can do is help them see that they still have skills which now need to be applied to different tasks and give them room to unfold their saga. Let that experience of their saga be vivid and fresh again, let them re-live the journey: the difficulties, worries, anxieties, that to them constituted almost an impossibility – and finally triumph, new life and new horizon. They could try to see the impact such a lived moment has upon their style of existence from the history-making of their times and the ferments of culture. They do this, not to find out what was wrong with their childhood, like in psychology, but to discover what enabled them to come through all these events and prevail.

This type of recounting serves two purposes: first, it teaches the younger generation that older people who refuse to be seduced by the culture's value system have the potential to be an exceptional prophetic force in the world and second, it allows the elderly brothers/sisters to re-live their triumphs, their joys and somehow see themselves as heroes, through the grace of God; for against all odds and in spite of all difficulties they persevered. For this reason it is necessary to incorporate the younger finally professed religious in such a formation course, so that they can learn.

Nevertheless, such a formation programme should also be flexible because it could be possible that a particular group prefers to consider with one another the doubts and fears that they are having at this stage of their lives, and their expectations from the community and from the younger generation. Recently, I became aware that some elderly religious would prefer to be called upon to make an assessment of the present generation and to use themselves as a paradigm for such findings. So in this case, the saga of their lives could take a move from here. To this effect, I assisted a course of this sort wherein four elderly religious, two women and two men, were called upon to give a seminar on their assessment on the young religious of their order. Each of them said something on the looseness of the younger generation giving a practical example and in turn narrated similar difficulties in their early stages of formation and how hard they laboured in order to stand firm against all odds. They also demonstrated how the contemporary culture is having a 'negative' influence on religious mentality. Let me illustrate this form of saga by reporting an anecdote of one of the priests.

> One of them a religious priest, while talking about the present generation's tendency for independence, told a very fascinating story of himself, how he had to learn in a hard way to be dependent. He said that all his life he had been an activist and for him, self-esteem was tied to self-reliance. Though he was a religious priest, he nevertheless had a considerable amount of independence and had been able to help many people in different ways. This service had given his life meaning and had also given him joy and fulfilment.
>
> His idea of life and of meaning was totally overturned when he had a terrible accident and was hospitalized. His first reaction to this condition was that he immediately became uncommunicative, immobile and resisted eating. It was rightly concluded that his condition was not the result of his physical problems, but was due to the shock of losing his freedom and privacy and suddenly becoming dependent on others for meeting his basic needs. He also said that he had always been able to speak freely about death and had tried all his life to get himself ready for death but, he had never been able to think of the possibility of receiving care from others or of moving into a full-care nursing home. It was apparent that his anxiety about helplessness

was greater than that about death. His own life had been a struggle for independence. He enjoyed giving to others and helping others. Now he was totally dependent upon receiving help from others. Little by little and over a period of several months, he said, it took him all the nerves in his body and his moral, mental and spiritual energies to begin to come to terms with his new situation. Increasingly he became able to accept his dependence and the care from others.

It is indeed captivating to hear how he was able to put this story into the saga of his life by bringing out the lessons he had learnt from it and how that had made of him a different person capable of giving and receiving love and care. He went on to say that for him this was a breakthrough of the Spirit and a realization of human spirit; that the transformation was in the direction of *becoming a centre of freedom and of love*. It is an example not only of the social character of spirit, but of what might be called the paradoxical character of that form of love we call *care*.

The fragile and dependent elderly religious brothers/sisters, even those who are confused and senile, have not lost all centre, he said, to be a centre is *not only* to give but also to receive, and those who cannot yet give or those who can no longer give, may yet give, in *receiving* care. For me, this point is wonderful. Being a centre or being at the

> centre is not only by giving but also by receiving. What is their gift one would ask? It is the gift of the newborn child, who by inviting and receiving love, yet paradoxically gives a form of love to the parents. So too, the dependent aging or the retarded brothers/sisters give in their receiving. They make possible a deepening and extension of spirit in the lives of those who care and in the community of those who care. Theirs is the gift of being open to caring love, of being able to receive such love. This too is a form of life in Christ or in the Spirit. Such life in the Spirit is as important for the nurture of the human spirit as the care-giving itself.
>
> When he fully recovered from his illness he became a different person. That experience of suffering transformed him. So, seeing the younger generation of religious who are just as he was many years ago, he understood them but he would like them to learn from his experience without going through what he went through.

Though the shift from a state of productivity and relative independence to a state of dependence in a society that has taught us to esteem ourselves in terms of productivity was not and still is not an easy one, yet we should understand our religious vocation as twofold. The first is about being and the second is about doing. Our being is not limited by our ability to do. Our core identity informs our calling and remains part of us no matter what our station or stage in life. The invitation at each stage in life is to discern how our unique calling will be expressed in this particular time and place and in light of our religious identity.

Each transition offers us new opportunities to grow deeper in God's love and to bless others in ways we had not imagined or thought possible. So the saga of one's life is a help to the elderly members; it inspires confidence 'that there is still more "life" to be "lived" and yet more heights to be scaled. The tragedy of advanced age is that so often, men and women cease to press towards the goal of their high calling. They cease learning, cease growing, they give up and resign from life. As wisdom dawns with age, we begin to measure our experiences not by what life gives to us, nor by the things withheld from us, but by their power to help us grow in spiritual wisdom.'[38]

Care of the Elderly Members of our Communities

Every passage to a new stage of growth implies a sort of positive disintegration of the personality which must then be rebuilt on a new basis. At this stage of the ongoing formation which continues till death, charity in the Mystical Body of Christ and for one's community and congregation should govern our attitude towards the aged members of our communities. For these elderly members of our communities, the type of formation they need at this stage is learning how to give by receiving care. Surely this is something that all of us have to learn over the entire course of our religious lives and which simply takes a new form and goes to the next level at this stage. This is an art which is not easy especially for those elderly members who were very active in their younger years. They were centres by giving; now they are asked to be centres by receiving.

However, what is necessary at this phase depends very much on the level of formation received earlier. Besides, their receiving care is also a witness of the Gospel and an act of charity on the community who give the care 'out of gratitude to them for offering their lives in service of the Church and society' and also in the hope that 'they continue to support the course of the Gospel through prayer, sacrifice and silent witness and enrich their Congregation with wisdom and experience'. In this way 'they deserve our continued respect and support.'[39]

The aged, the feeble and the sick are all members of the Mystical Body of Christ, and we must see Christ in them, since in them Christ becomes visible. There is no giving up work in the Mystical Body, no pensioning of its members. On the contrary, the old become more the object of care and love, the weaker they are. In the words of St Paul, the Apostle to the Gentiles, no member can say to the other:

> I have no need of you. … it is those that seem

> the more feeble members of the body that are the more necessary, and those that we think the less honourable members of the body we surround with more abundant honour. … But God has so tempered the body together … that there may be no disunion in the body, but that the members may have care for one another. And if one member suffers anything, all the members suffer with it, or if one member glories, all the members rejoice with it. Now you are the body of Christ, member for member. (1 Corinthians 12:21-27)

The aged people are sometimes, perhaps unconsciously, hard with regard to their little demands, their innocent manias, wrinkles that time has impressed on their souls, like those that furrow their faces, but that should make them more venerable in the eyes of others. People are easily inclined to reprove them for what they no longer do, instead of reminding them again, as they deserve, of what they *have* done. One smiles, perhaps, at their weakening memory, and one does not always recognize the wisdom of their judgements. In their eyes, blurred by tears, you will look in vain for the flame of enthusiasm, but you can see the light of resignation in which there already burns the desire of eternal splendour.[40] These aged members are the visible sinned against we have in our midst. We are to be their voice and start to minister compassion to them.

5. *Religious Transformation*

Discovering the etymology of the word *transformation* gives us a better understanding of what it implies. The word *transformation* is made up of two Latin words, *trans* and *forma,* where *trans* could mean 'across, over, on the other side'. *Forma* means form. The two together would literally mean 'a change of form' and, according to its use, it could refer to any type of change, as for instance, a change of character, or of clothing style, or even more importantly of consciousness.[41] It can also mean a change of perspective or an inward spiritual change, also called conversion. Religious formation is interested in the last two. It is obvious that ordinary human transformation is an activity of the self. But spiritual transformation is a result of the transforming activity of the Holy Spirit. Religious transformation is radically focused upon the personal saving presence of Christ as the largely-hidden but ever-present Source and Destiny of transformation itself. Because of this, no amount of formation transforms.

Transformation is the work of God. James Loder states: 'Transforming moments need to be recognized as sources of a new knowledge about God, self, and world as generating the quality and strength of life that can deal creatively with the sense of nothingness shrouding the extremities and pervading the mainstream of modern living.'[42] The encounter with Jesus Christ is the central, enduring, and necessary key to transformation. Loder focuses on what he calls 'convictional experiences' – life-changing events, often sudden, through which ways of knowing, believing, feeling, and acting are radically changed. But before this experience brings a sudden and radical change there must be a conscious 'scanning'. This kind of transformation has formation as an aid to disposition for it, but the kind of transformation which necessarily comes by means of religious formation is what is called transformational learning.

Transformational Learning

The type of learning that is done during religious formation both initial and ongoing formation is called transformational learning. This is so because this type of learning has far-reaching consequences on personality more than any other kind of learning. It is a learning experience that shapes the learner and produces a significant impact to the point of affecting the learner's subsequent experiences. In a transformational learning process one's 'meaning perspective' changes. 'Meaning perspective' refers to one's overall world view, which comprises knowledge, values and beliefs, one's stance towards earthly realities and one's system of behaviour. Usually one's meaning perspective is passively formed right through one's life experiences in childhood, during the youthful years and in young adulthood. These elements serve as a filter in perceiving the present reality and in determining how to organize and interpret one's current experiences. Through the process of formation and ongoing formation the religious acquires self-knowledge and, by rational discourse and critical reflection, explores the depth and meaning of the elements that make up his/her worldview in order to produce a more inclusive worldview. The success of the outcome is rated by the development of greater autonomy as a person,[43] which in a way also defines the condition of adulthood.

Transformational learning can be attained only to the extent that one uses the tools of critical reflection and rational discourse in order to arrive at a self-knowledge that is total, deep and long-lasting. In the same vein it should be added that this transformational learning reorganizes one's perspective and should seriously affect the intimacy of relationship and vision that one has of God and other spiritual realities (the role that the life of the spirit has on the individual). 'The full development of religious values and Christian sanctity in a soul is inconceivable if a man does not start out with a healthy mind, well balanced in its activities.'[44] This affirmation seems to imply that any deficiency in mental health would be an obstacle to full spiritual development. It further assumes that psychological growth and spiritual growth are interrelated. The greater the psychological maturity acquired, the greater are the possibilities for spiritual development.

Sources of Transformation

Spiritual transformation takes place when the human person collaborates with God's grace. There are many sources present in one's whole formative life which transform and predispose a person for transformation. There are five major sources, and with their assistance one is capable of a profound spiritual transformation being open to the action of God. The following are the five powerful sources for spiritual transformation:

1. Holy Scripture which not only teaches the religious but also transforms him/her in his/her daily contact with it. The Word of God has played an important role in the personal lives of many saints down through the centuries. A prayerful listening to the Scriptures opens one's heart to hear not only words about God, but words from God, hence the importance of *Lectio Divina*. The Holy Spirit also plays an important role in understanding the Scriptures.

2. The Rule/Constitution and the *Charism*: This is God's special gift to a religious institute for the good of the Church, and if honestly and authentically lived, it also brings about a gradual formation and transformation. It is the Holy Spirit's way of showing the richness of the mysteries of Christ. The Rule/Constitution or/and the *Charism* of a religious congregation is in a way Scripture abridged. In as much as in them some part of the Gospel message

and values are highlighted, they therefore possess in them potentials for transformation.

3. Apostolate: In Mark 3:14, we are told that 'he appointed twelve; they were to be *his companions* and *to be sent out* to preach.' The two parts of the process of being a disciple of Christ are enumerated in this passage. The first part involves union with Christ, or centering one's life on Christ, and the second part is the involvement in the mission, which consists in proclaiming Jesus to others and serving Jesus in others. In this sense, the apostolate also has its place in the spiritual transformation of the religious, because it demands a union with the Lord before involvement in service. It is the intensity of one's closeness with the Lord that will render fruitful one's apostolate and activities exercised in the service of others. It is a profound union with the Lord that enables one to communicate and confirm, with his/her life, the message of Christ to humanity in a language that can be convincing.

4. Sacraments: The sacraments are channels of grace and the most powerful sources for the spiritual growth and maturity of the consecrated person. In a particular way the Eucharist becomes the heart of spiritual transformation. Religious are able to nourish their lives from this central sacrament of Christian life. Above all, the Eucharist brings about communion with Christ and strengthens the commitment of the

religious. Confession and the Eucharist ought to be, especially for the consecrated person, irreplaceable instruments of purification, strength, illumination and union with God.

5. The Cross: Another true but sometimes very difficult means of transformation is formation in the cross. A religious should learn to expect and welcome trials in his/her religious calling and flourish in spite of it, whether the surroundings where he/she finds him/herself is agreeable or not. Accepting the cross both forms and transforms in the process. Since religious life is a memory of Christ's life on earth, the cross is therefore a sign of its authenticity.

The Paradox of Formation and Transformation

'Without the long process of formation, there could be no transformation; yet no amount of careful formation can transform.'[45] In this contradictory-but-true statement, Rosemary Haughton has addressed a key challenge to Religious life. Here in the form of a mystery lies one of the continuing core challenges of religious formators, i.e., 'no amount of formation can transform.' Then one wonders and asks the need for all the years of formation if such a statement is indeed true. What do we hope to achieve with such when we are sure that no matter how it is done or how many years we put into it, it will not bring about the transformation of life?

Envisioning the Connection between Formation and Transformation

Rosemary Haughton stresses the complete separateness of formation and transformation. She uses the analogy of a circle and a contiguous tangent. The circle represents in this view the extent of formation or chronological time while the tangent represents transformational or *kairotic* time. The only way that the tangent can actually touch the circle is through a magnetic arcing of a power cantered in the tangent. It is through the power of this completely-un-expectable and essentially 'timeless' arcing that the 'flashpoint' of transformation happens. In other words, Haughton is telling us that both the boundary line (which is transformation in *kairotic* time) and the circle (which in turn is the formation that takes place chronologically) are in a very close proximity but contact or touching is not possible. This boundary line (contiguous tangent) possesses a magnetic power that acts like a spark which eventually makes contact or touching possible thereby bringing about transformation.

This magnetic arcing or what I call a spark is the grace of God which unexpectedly touches the soul predisposed by the chronological circles of formation. Haughton went on to explain that 'transformation is a timeless point of decision, yet it can only operate in the personality formed through the time-conditioned stages of development, and its effects can only be worked out in terms of that formation.'[46] The transforming meeting-point (tangent) momentarily touches the edge of this circle made possible in part through a 'timeless' decision, but most fully through the grace of God's transforming presence. This 'flashpoint' can only be interpreted through the 'time-conditioned stages of development.'

Drawing from this analogy then, we are meant to understand that: first, while both formation and transformation are necessary, neither is sufficient. Second, the transformational line may appear to be strictly peripheral, but its fullest significance can only be grasped at the very centre of the formational circle. The essentially strange-but-true riddle that lies behind the paradox of formation and transformation rests with the question of constancy and change.[47] In both formation and transformation there are constancy and change and there are also stages. In religious formation the stages are empirical (or rather external) in the sense that we all see the candidate going through certain stages like from being an aspirant to pre-postulant and from there to Postulate, and then into the Novitiate and into being a professed member of the community. After a minimum period of three years and a maximum period of nine years, he/she takes final vows. So also in transformation there are changes but these changes are more or less internal, the final stage is what externally becomes evident.

Stages of Spiritual Transformation

The process always begins in a conflict or rather in a sudden realization that something is wrong. Conflict initiates the knowing response, but this is followed by an 'interlude for scanning'. During this interlude a search takes place (both consciously and unconsciously) for possible solutions and for deeper understandings of the problem. It is 'the step of waiting, wondering, following hunches, and exhausting the possibilities.'[48] This period may be long or brief before acknowledgement comes. Some call this waiting period a desert experience, when one has to struggle to let go of things. The price of letting go is very high because there is insecurity and uncertainty. Sooner or later it is followed by, almost intruded upon by, a 'constructive act of the imagination; an insight, intuition, or vision appears on the border between the conscious and the unconscious, usually with convincing force, and conveys in a form readily available to consciousness, the essence of the resolution.'[49]

Self-surrender to God is the next important stage. In that situation of struggle, the individual feels the need for an unconditional and total abandonment to God. It is a difficult stage, but peace flows once one surrenders. This surrender to God includes a renunciation of all delusion, of false images of self, of an exaggerated assessment of one's capabilities. By giving in to God's will, one finds peace. The resolution has two immediate effects. First, the energy bound up in sustaining the conflict is released. One feels freed and unburdened. Second, the individual is opened to God and therefore to self and to the world. He/she feels a more deep, intimate, lucid contact with both self and environment. The final movement in the sequence of transformation is interpretation. One interprets the conflict in the light of its resolution, and vice versa. One interprets one's whole discovery in some public form to others and this is the stage where it becomes manifest. In a word, the final stage of spiritual transformation is integration. Integration means the capacity to unite all the aspects of life, even in the midst of one's struggles. Fundamentally, it is a call to reality, or to radicalism. Total spiritual transformation is in this radical reorganization of one's life. In a word it is a conscious awareness of having surrendered to the stirring of the Spirit.

So in the religious formation which is characteristically 'ongoing' and continuous, the candidate though at a point (after the final vows) no longer goes through an external change, yet the formative process continues, because he/she continues to grow in the knowledge of God and in the knowledge of his/her congregation. In the same way we continue to be transformed by the renewal of our minds that we may prove what is the will of God, what is good and acceptable and perfect (Romans 12:2).

Besides, this little expository should offer us some guidelines in a continuing search for an understanding of the paradox of formation and transformation. We can better grasp why 'no amount of careful formation can transform' since:

- Formation itself is not possible without the all-encompassing, central and essential role which the transformative processes play.
- Formation has an inherent force of fragmentation, hence the person being formed goes through different stages of formation.
- One is formed in something specific, like in the religious life the candidate is formed by being redirected into the rules for living the life in a specific community or congregation.
- Formation cannot properly be understood as unilateral and irreversible; instead it is and must be somehow continuous and ongoing.

Alternately, we can now better grasp the wisdom of the first half of this paradox, i.e., 'without the long process of formation, there could be no transformation.' Since:

Formation here must be understood in the first place not in the sense of an activity exercised by a human formator on another person, but as a gradual and constant transformation, never fully realized, of a person who using the means offered in his/her formation programme, allows the Holy Spirit to restore within him/her the marred image of God.

Transformation must be interpreted within the

context of a lifelong, unending (if not endless!) and at least potentially universal process called formation.

There are inherent continuities which must of necessity bind our experiences in formation together; no transformation can undo this continuity

Transformation, like all other phenomena, must eventually submit to the test of empiricism and the stage theory (the different stages in both formation and transformation) aid us significantly in this task.

Finally, both formation and transformation must acknowledge their inherent limits, if we are to bring their full circle back into the compass of the practice of the religious formators.

All these point to the fact that religious formation is not necessarily meant to achieve a spiritual transformation but it disposes the candidate for it. From the spiritual point of view it should be pointed out that transformation is primarily attributed to the grace of God, but it also involves human cooperation, which comes about through a formation in transformational learning. In this sense, transformation could also be called conversion.[50] The deeper and more authentic the experience, the more profound are the changes in the person. It is difficult for one who has had a true experience to resist change. In the same way it could be said that it is difficult to change one's life if significant experiences are absent.[51] We are particularly fortunate to have the journal of the late Secretary General of the United Nations, Dag

Hammarskjöld (Markings). His, was an example of a transformational self-surrender. What could be a more vivid account of religious conversion than this entry from Pentecost, 1961: 'I don't know Who – or what – put the question, I don't know when it was put. I don't even remember answering. But at some moment I did answer Yes to Someone – or Something – and from that hour I was certain that existence is meaningful and that, therefore, my life, in self-surrender, had a goal.'[52] Thus one sees that whatever threatens to deplete us can be used by God as a source of transformation to new hope and courage. Such events remind us that the potency to start again may be contingent upon our willingness to step aside and appraise in humility who we are and what our purpose in life really is. It is to describe it in language that everyone can understand, in terms of what De Caussade calls 'the sacrament of the present moment'.

> To discover God just as clearly in very minor or ordinary things as in the big things of life is to have a far from ordinary faith. It is to have one that is great and extraordinary. To be satisfied with the present moment is to relish and adore the divine will moving through all that we have to do and suffer as events crowd in upon us.[53]

A spiritual person therefore, is one who has decided to respond to God's call, which he/she has experienced, and then strives to make that call the centre of activity and of choice. In other words, the call becomes the integrating factor for that person. Hence, the truth that spiritual life becomes the work of a lifetime can be re-emphasized. Spiritual transformation is the consistent conviction of the ever-abiding presence of God rather than a particular experience or even a set of experiences. It is a restructuring of one's consciousness in which the divine reality is perceived to be always present. One can grow towards physical adulthood merely by continuing to breathe, but more is required of emotional development and maturity and much more is required of full spiritual development. It is not by simply *knowing* God that one is transformed, but by being fully united with him in the company of the brethren that one reaches one's ultimate destiny.

Notes

1 On 12th August 1980, the Congregation for Religious and Secular Institutes published a document; *Religious and Human Promotion*, which was a result of the work of the Plenary of the 25-28 April 1978. Among other things, the document presented a general criteria for discernment (nn. 13-31) and as a guide or general criteria for the discernment 'four great fidelities' were proposed: *Fidelity to man and to our time; Fidelity to Christ and to the Gospel; Fidelity to the Church and to its mission in the world; Fidelity to religious life and to the charism of one's own institute* (n. 13). The arrangement of these 'four great fidelities' or the document as a whole bears the sign of its historical content that is why in some point it was successively reviewed and improved. Concretely, the frame of the 'four great fidelities' was later reordered and clarified. The latter reordering of the four fidelities also correspond to the present historical changes.

2 Cf. C. NANNI, 'Formazione', in J. M. PRELLEZO - C. NANNI - G. MALIZIA (eds.), *Dizionario delle Scienze dell'Educazione,* Elle Di Ci: Leumann Turin 1997, p. 432.

3 Roger BALDUCELLI, O.S.F.S., 'The Decision for Celibacy', in: *Theological Studies* 36 No 21, 1975, pp. 219-242, here p. 219.

4 See Roger BALDUCELLI, O.S.F.S., 'The Decision for Celibacy', p. 220.

5 Roger BADLDUCELLI, O.S.F.S., 'The Decision for Celibacy', p. 221.

6 Apostolic Exhortation *Patores Dabo Vobis,* of St John Paul II, 1992

7 Edward FARLEY, Ecclesial Man, Philadelphia 1975, read pp. 132-133. For a phenomenological description of this situation see also chapter 6 of this book.

8 Read Bénézet BUJO, Foundations of an African Ethics. Beyond the universal claims of Western Morality, The Cross Road Publishing Company, New York, 2001, p.4. Though it has generally been believed that *cognatus ergo sum* is an African Ethics because of the African community sense of existence but whether it is consciously or unconsciously acknowledged *cognatus ergo sum* is a universal reality.

9 Aubrey HODES, Encounter with Martin Buber, London, 1972, p. 217.

10 Dolores HART & Richard DENEUT, The Ear of the Heart. An Actress' Journey from Hollywood to Holy Vows, Ignatius Press, San Francisco 2013, p. 318.

11 Timothy RADCLIFFE, Sing a New Song: The Christian Vocation, Dominican publications Dublin, 2000, p. 175.

12 Timothy RADCLIFFE, Sing a New Song, p.173.

13 S 358A.1; PLS 2:671-2; trans. Edmund Hill, The Sermons of Saint Augustine Brooklyn: New City 3/10:196; hereafter Sermons.

14 Augustine De Mor. Eccl. Cath. 27.53; PL 32:1333.

15 Timothy RADCLIFFE, Sing a New Song, p. 181.

16 Cf. Timothy RADCLIFFE, Sing a New Song, p.181.

17 *Facticity,* is a concept described by Sartre in Being and Nothingness. For him, *facticity* was the set of facts relevant or given to the person, for example his physical characteristics, his parents, and his unique position. It represents the contingency of human existence and belongs to being-in-itself . According

to Sartre, this finitude of human existence does not determine our freedom or our fundamental project. Instead, it is the basis upon which we make our free choices. An infinite being does not need to exercise choice, and human choice consists precisely in discovering a person's *facticity* and seeking to negate or surpass its limitations. Read Jean-Paul SARTRE, Being and Nothingness: an essay in Phenomenological Ontology, Citadel Press 2001.

18 Reported by Timothy RADCLIFFE, Sing a New Song, p. 176.

19 Letter to Stefano di Codiponte, 22 May 1492, cited by Timothy RADCLIFFE, Sing a New Song, p.174.

20 See the Chapter on Community life for these different dimensions.

21 It is important to note that this point has long been stressed by the 1990 Document on religious formation *Potissimum Institutioni* (PI) No 16b, it says that the programme of formation 'should be well structured and harmonious, include fundamental elements of Sacred Scripture, spiritual theology, moral theology, ecclesiology, theology and the law of religious life - in particular of each of the evangelical counsels - liturgy, and also fundamental concepts of anthropology and psychology which should give to the novice, at the beginning of the formative journey, the possibility of knowing himself or herself better, particularly in those areas most needing formation. These subjects should be treated as contributors to formation.'

22 Angel PARDILLA, 'Theological Identity of Religious Life', in: *INFORMATIONES s.c.r.i.s. (Sacra Congregazione per i Religiosi e gli Istituti Secolari),* Anno XII, n. 1 giugno 1986, pp. 260-279, here p.264.

23 Religious and Human Advancement, January 1981, No. 7 in Vatican Council II, Vol. 2, p.267. A. FLANNERY, (ed.).

24 Congregation for the Institute of Consecrated Life and Societies of Apostolic Life, Starting Afresh from Christ: A Renewed Commitment to Consecrated Life in the Third Millenium, 14 June 2002, No 15

25 This life-style pattern is well explained and elaborated by James E. LODER in his article 'The Fashioning of Power: A Christian Perspective on the Life-Style Phenomenon', in: A. J. MCKELWAY and E. David WILLIS, eds., *The Context of Contemporary Theology,* Atlanta: John Knox, 1974, pp. 187-205. Loder uses the phrase, 'Socially acceptable patterns of self-destruction', which I modify here. See p. 187.

26 James E. LODER, 'The Fashioning of Power', p. 187.

27 Nelson MANDELA, The Long Walk to Freedom, London 1994, p. 750.

28 http://www.scourmont.be/Armand/writings/formation.htm.

29 James E. LODER, 'The Fashioning of Power', p. 191.

30 Edward FARLEY, Ecclesial Man, Philadelphia 1975, p. 141.

31 E. GAMBARI, Religious Life. According to Vatican II and The New Code of Canon Law St Paul Editions: Boston 1986, p. 250.

32 Cf. K. MCALPIN, 'Conversion. A Summons from the Word of God', in: *Review for Religious* 61 2002 1, p. 49.

33 Cf. Sante. BISIGNANO, 'Itinerario di formazione alla vita religiosa', in: *COLLECTION*, *Vita consacrata un dono del Signore alla sua Chiesa* (Elle Di Ci: Leumann Turin 1994), p. 314.

34 Cf. Sante BISIGNANO, 'La formazione permanente linee fondamentali, criterie itinerari', in: *COLLECTION*, *La formazione permanente nella vita religiosa* (Editrice Rogate: Rome 1984), pp. 54-55.

35 See Dolores HART & Richard DENEUT, The Ear of the Heart. An Actress' Journey from Hollywood to Holy Vows, p. 316-317.

36 Ross SYNDER, 'Religious Meaning and the latter third of Life', in: *Religious Education* 76, 5 1981, pp. 534-552, here p. 534.

37 Ross SYNDER, 'Religious Meaning and the latter third of Life', p. 535.

38 Evelyn SENGE, Quaker Faith and Practice: The Yearly Meeting of the Religious Society of Friends, London 1999, Personal journey Section 21:45.

39 Bishop Lucius Iwejuru UGORJI, DMMM at 50: Witnessing to God's Mercy. A sermon on the occasion of the Golden Jubilee Celebration of the DMMM Sisters, Lumen Press Umuahia, 2011, pp. 15-16.

40 See the Address to married couples, July 14, 1950, quoted in *The Pope Speaks,* compiled by Michael Chinigo, Pantheon, 1957, pp. 72-74.

41 Cf. M. STEIN, Transformation. Emergence of the Self, A & M University Press: Laredo 1998, p. 51; see also: B. BAYNHAM, 'Transformation,' in M. DOWNEY (ed.), *The New Dictionary of Catholic Spirituality* (Liturgical Press: Collegeville 1993), p. 967.

42 James LODER, The Transforming Moment, San Francisco Harper & Row 1981, p. viii.

43 Cf. J. MEZIROW, Transformative Dimension of Adult Learning Jossey- Bass: San Francisco 1991 pp. 145-146.

44 M.J. O'BRIEN - R.J. STEIMEL, Psychological Aspects of Spiritual Development The Catholic University of America Press: Washington 1965), p. 23.

45 Rosemary HAUGHTON, 'Formation and Transformation', in: *Conversion: Perspectives on Personal and Social Transformation,* ed. Walter Conn New York: Alba House, 1978, p. 25

46 Rosemary HAUGHTON, 'Formation and Transformation', p. 25.

47 There are two sharply differing alternative views on this question. The first one is best represented by the early Greek philosopher, Heraclitus (535-457 B.C.). Plato quotes Heraclitus as stating, 'Nothing endures but change.' See John Bartlett, *Familiar Quotations,* ed. Emily Beck (Boston: Little, Brown, and Co., 1968), p. 77. The contrasting view is represented by the nineteenth century author, Alphonse Karr (1808-1875), 'The more things change, the more they remain the same.', John Bartlett, *Familiar Quotations* p. 627. From this radically opposing vantage point, change only discloses the enduring sameness of things. Heinz Werner's theory of human development proposed to reconcile these radically opposing viewpoints on constancy and change. Werner's leading interpreter, Jonas Langer sees the following question standing at the heart of Werner's concern. That is: 'How does a developing organism change qualitatively, and at the same time, preserve its integrity?', Jonas Langer, Werner's Comparative Organismic Theory, in: Carmichae Ts Manual of Child Psychology, ed. Paul M. Müssen, 3rd ed. New York John Wiley, 1970, p. 733. The question here is how we account for the continuities of our personhood in the face of the discontinuities of qualitative change. In short, how does the formational process retain its integrity while being transformed?

48 James LODER, The Transforming Moment, p.32.

49 Ibid.

50 Cf. B. BAYNHAM, 'Transformation,' in M. DOWNEY (Ed.), *The New Dictionary of Catholic Spirituality* (Liturgical Press: Collegeville 1993), p. 967.

51 Cf. E. ALBERICH - J. VALLABARAJ, *Communicating a Faith that Transforms. Handbook of Fundamental Catechetics* (Kristu Jyoti Publications: Bangalore 2004), p. 77.

52 Dag Hammarskjöld, Markings by Alfred A. KNOPF, New York 1964, p. 205

53 J. P. De Caussade, Abandonment to Divine Providence, trans. John Beevers. New York: Image Books, 1975, p. 39.

IV

COMMUNION

THE 1983 CODE OF CANON LAW distinguishes religious institutes from secular institutes and societies of apostolic life. Whereas members of secular institutes bind themselves by sacred bonds but do not necessarily live in common (Can 714), and members of societies of apostolic life live in common but do not take religious vows (Can 712, 714), members of religious institutes pronounce public vows and also live a fraternal life in common (Can 607 n. 2). The *fraternal life in common and the public vows* of the members are thus seen by the new Code as essential elements of religious life, distinguishing it from life in a secular institute and in a society of apostolic life. This is fully in line with the historical tradition of religious life as we saw in chapter one of this work and with the teaching of *Lumen Gentium* and *Perfectae Caritatis.*

1. Community Life as Lived by the Early Christians

The early Christians we were told: 'shared the faith, owned everything in common … with one heart, they regularly went to the temple but met in their houses for the breaking of bread; they shared their food gladly and generously; they praised God and were looked up to by everyone. Day by day the Lord added to their community those destined to be saved' (Acts 2:44-47). Community life in order to be a success presumes an enormous amount of trust in each other: the apostles were trusted to use these blessings faithfully; those in need were trusted to speak truthfully about their needs. Without this mutual trust and mutual truthfulness, holding all things in common cannot work. This is why when Ananias and Sapphira failed to truthfully declare their possessions and lay them at the feet of the apostles, the response from God was terrifying. Truthfulness is the centre and heart of the unity and trust that underlie a community life in which believers hold all things in common. The Acts of the Apostles makes it clear that this unity and trust is a fragile achievement which depends on truthfulness. It does not, however, depend on moral perfection. The oneness of mind and heart characteristic of the early Christians is not the result of sinlessness, but of being a reconciled and reconciling people. Thus, truthfulness can only flourish if a community's practices of forgiveness and reconciliation are in good working order. Religious Communities can only learn to speak in the ways envisioned in Acts 4-6 when they are able to speak truthfully about their imperfections or sins and realize that their failings need not ultimately destroy their relationship with God and others.

2. The implications of Community Life as spelt out in the Code:

- The members are united into 'as it were, a special family in Christ' (Can 602). This family is based on faith and the members do not choose one another instead they were brought together by God to be an effective sign of love between the Father and Son within the Trinity.
- This fraternal life should be defined in such a way that it grows to be a mutual support in fulfilling their vocation (Can 602). It is not enough that religious are together under the same roof. Particular laws should indicate how this mutual assistance is to be effectively given and received.
- Firmly rooted and based in God's pardoning love, the fraternal union of the religious is to be an example of universal reconciliation in Christ (Can 602). Religious community should be a place in which pardon is daily given and received, a clear sign that God reconciles people to himself, appealing to us to be reconciled (cf. 2 Corinthians 5:18-21).

- Every community is under the authority of a superior (Can 608), who resides in the house (Can 629). 'Superiors are to exercise their power, received from God through the ministry of the Church, in a spirit of service' (Can 618). Every community shall have a superior, a human and frail spiritual head, who however unworthily 'holds the place of God' (PC 14).
- The institute supplies the members of all that they need in order to fulfil the purpose of their vocation (Can 670). On the other hand all that a religious acquires by personal labour or on behalf of the institute belongs to the institute. This applies to pensions, grants, and insurances, unless the institute's own laws decree otherwise (Can 668 n. 3). These provisions regarding temporal goods and the practice of religious poverty aim at consolidating the sense of community.

The idea behind the provisions listed above is the belief that in and through their compassionate shared living, members of a religious community are unanimously seeking for an 'extra quality' or rather to go an extra mile so that together they may stand out as a visible sign of God's inner Trinitarian life.

3. Theological Dimensions of Community Life

The Second Vatican Council with its Dogmatic Constitution on the Church *Lumen Gentium* has developed an Ecclesiology of *Communio,* that is also very useful for the theology of religious life. Religious community is a Church *communio* with all its theological contents. It is essentially a place where those called to a shared *charism* seek together the will of God. It is also a place of emotional and affective growth, because the Christian community embodies a new way of looking at human relationships. Religious life also enhances a deep relationship with God and eventually is practically lived as a sacramental expression of the mystery of the Church.

There are four dimensions to Religious Community:

1. *Theological reality*: Religious embody and witness the dimension of the universal Christian call to unity in Christ, the transcendent quality of Christian community as an eschatological reality. In being called to enter a religious community, the choice is not made based on biological, national, ethnic, racial, political or economic considerations. A Religious commits him/herself through the vows to a unity that has no natural 'glue' in order to witness to the possibility and reality of the transcendent unity made possible by Christ on the Cross of Calvary.
2. The religious community is a *Spiritual reality*: There is a strong sense of 'belonging' to a religious institute/community/Order. For example, I am not just a member of the Benedictine Order or family, but I am a Benedictine. What does that mean? It means that if

the Benedictine community identity does not deeply colour my religious sense of self before God, before my fellow human beings and in the world, then I do not spiritually belong to the Benedictine religious Order regardless of my lifestyle and my wearing their religious habit. 'Benedictine' in a way is my ecclesial surname. That is why we proudly add it at the end of our names, Fr/Br/Sr … OSB. Quite often the togetherness of the members of a community might not be necessary but the individual must carry the community into every experience and commitment of their lives.

3. The religious community is a *ministerial reality*: here we talk of corporateness, the unity in diversity of the congregation's mission and ministries. A religious in ministry is not a solitary or private agent. In whatever apostolate or mission one finds oneself, that mission is always exercised in the name of the congregation. A practical demonstration of this reality is when a congregation has two of its members engaged in an apostolate in a diocese. The congregation automatically claims that 'we are in so-and-so diocese', they do not say Br/Sr X and X are in so-and-so diocese but 'we', that is the congregation.

4. *Psychological and social*: this is an affective reality. The religious foregoes the personal support and the resources for growth from his/her natural family. Consequently, they ought to find in their communities personal acceptance, encouragement in prayer and

ministry, affirmation and support in times of success and failure. They should be ready and able to accept constructive challenge and assistance when necessary.

To belong to a community is not a title but a claim on the care of those with whom one has decided to spend one's entire life. This mutual caring should be effectively fostered in communities. However, life in community is not always easy but that too, is part of the challenges of religious life. God calls a variety of individuals with different backgrounds and personalities to a common place and or purpose in which they live together and form community.

Each person whom God sends, despite his/her needs and weaknesses, is a gift to the community. Each of us is meant to grow into what God would have us be, that unique person made in His image, conflicts and misunderstandings notwithstanding. 'Conflict, indeed, is never far from the presence of Christ in the gospels, and in a religious community, often contrary to appearances, it is never very far away either.'[1] The call to live in community, the call to commit to God and to live the life of the Gospel is a challenge to all who receive vocation to the religious life today just as it was in ages past.

To answer that call may take us many places we never dreamed of going, to do things we never imagined we could do and to live each day in an unexpected way. Religious life could therefore be rightly described as an adventure. When in our communities we share in Christ's ministry, we also share in his passion and grace. For that very reason, 'whoever enters into a religious community, whoever perpetually and irrevocably makes this way of life his own, chooses for himself an unforeseeable destiny. For the consequences of such an election and dedication to the community and its rationale of action cannot be foreseen in detail. And these consequences can be difficult and painful. But this gamble (considered in its formal structure) is involved in every human obligation, whereby another person with his own proper will becomes an inseparable part of one's own life.'[2]

Community: a Place of Forgiveness

Community life is a sacrament of God's compassionate love if and in so far as it embodies the saving reality of universal reconciliation in Christ. Religious community life can very frequently embody the reality of God's pardon precisely because it is often itself hard and burdened by conflict, and so calls for reconciliation. Once the religious grasps the fact that God is merciful they are freed to forgive and become agents of reconciliation.

Community is a privileged place for forgiveness. Inevitably, when persons live close to each other, their words will inflict wound on one another and their susceptibilities will clash; but the grace of God will enable the members of an ecclesial community to forgive and start afresh. So instead of projecting on to community unrealistically high expectations, or disliking community life or escaping from it on the pretext that it is better to go one's own way in order to survive and function apostolically, the religious will come to realize that the community is a gift that leads one deep into the mystery of forgiveness. 'If we come into community without knowing that the reason we come is to discover the mystery of forgiveness, we will soon be disappointed.'[3] Because God is a God of compassion, a community is God-like, if it can rise to the heights of being a place of forgiveness where hurts are healed and relations of love and trust are created anew.

Religious Community Life is Different from Common Life

I would like to make this paragraph more concrete by making a sharp contrast between community life and common life. Oftentimes the term *community* and *common life* are used interchangeably, but they are not synonymous. Community is derived from the Latin word *communis* meaning *common*, which encompasses not only those who live a common life, but also those who have common identities, common works, common interests, common goal and common membership. Common life is included as one of the definitions of community, but community does not imply, necessarily, common life. In community life sharing and caring is seen and experienced in celebration, feasting, mourning and rejoicing at the very deeper level of our human relationship.

Community life is commitment to shared life expressed in the willingness to foster corporate life and mission at great cost to oneself even when not sharing the same address. While 'common life' may be defined as living under the same roof, community life is integral to religious existence and therefore an 'essential element' of such a life. Surprisingly, a richly textured communal spirit is absent in many religious congregations. Though there may be experiences of social togetherness and friendliness, yet if it remained only at this level it is what is called common life, which is however not the same as participating in and being deeply entwined within a spiritually grounded community. The two should not be confused. Inhabiting the same convent, eating together, occasionally praying together and so on is not the same as belonging to a community where your presence truly matters to others and their presence truly matters to you. That is to say: outwardly, members of a religious congregation because of their different apostolates may have little in common, i.e. they may often not be able to eat together nor always pray together, but inwardly, they can be touched by the possibility that they have something to learn from each other: broad friendship, mutuality of purpose and an abiding care for one another are all by-products of a spiritually grounded religious community that is working together.

The way in which members of a religious congregation reproduce the love of God through genuine hospitality and a love and care for one another will indicate whether they are indeed the body of Christ or simply a religious club. Uniformity does not constitute biblical community; neither does it favour religious community. If anything, it threatens it. Indeed, what is considered seriously wrong with 'common life' is not in the life-style of such a life but more in the absence of that fundamentally important psycho-social-spiritual unity of minds and heart in Christ, which is theologically essential to Christian life as such and to which religious life is explicitly committed to bear a particular witness.

Community Life: A Social Network that makes Fidelity to the Vows Possible

Community life is central and important to living the vows. The three evangelical vows are in turmoil today because the community dimension of the religious life is also in turmoil. One wonders why community living has so frequently become a gathering of strangers who meet occasionally for meals, take turns in cooking, attend stipulated meetings where they share what they must, but otherwise pass each other like ships in the night, busy about their ministries and apostolates but getting slowly and steadily evermore dehydrated except for the occasional reinforcement that comes from ministry support groups or from perhaps annual retreats. Why has community life for many of us become something that must be 'suffered' either because of ministry location or travel convenience, rather than something that empowers and affirms the vision of our constitutions?

It is not true that community is primarily fostered by what we do in it, with how many we are who live in it and with how often we meet etc. These issues are important but not central. The four necessary elements in building up a solid community living are:

- Mutual trust, (like we saw in the case of the early Christians in Acts)
- Vulnerability (readiness to receive and accept wounds and seek for reconciliation)
- To be poor in each other's presence (vulnerability; open to criticism and being open to sharing informations about one another)
- Above all openness to the self-revelation of God

A solid community living helps people invest their lives and confidence in one another for the sake of a common dream and a shared mission. The Gospel itself provides continuous clues for demonstrating how people who are very different can be drawn together to appreciate one another, to care for one another and to be there for one another. When in a community a brother/sister is always on the way and never in the community. Have you ever for a day said to him/her when you see him/her passing by you, 'Brother Joseph or Sister Irene, I miss you, I wish I could go out for dinner with you some day.' Or, 'I wish we can stay together and chat.' Perhaps one of the reasons why he/she is never there could be because he/she never felt missed by anybody. You have to let him/her know that you care.

A religious community where the individuals trust one another in spite of the inevitable human betrayals of one another; a community where mutual forgiveness and reconciliation are at home is a community that has a shared sense of grace, a community capable of sustaining Christian virtue. The members of such a religious community breathe together as the people of God and are capable of 'conspiring together'.[4]

Let me illustrate this point of caring, missing and being missed by one another with an experience: I travelled once to a particular community in a foreign country and in that community I knew only one sister whom I met some years back. She happened also to be the only one in that community who could speak English. Just three weeks after I had arrived she came to me to tell me that she was to move over to another community in another country. Oh Gosh! I couldn't bear it, I nearly cried but I managed to hold myself. I said to her: 'Sister, I will really miss you.' I sincerely meant it because I had no one to talk with even though I was to learn the language but that normally comes with time. Anyway, to my greatest surprise, this sister burst out crying. I was shocked and some of the other sisters in the community came to find out what was wrong. A few days later before this sister travelled, she came to me again and told me her story; that since she joined the community no one had ever missed her and that she felt her presence was superfluous and that was why she made up her mind to leave. She went on to narrate all the tragic experiences she had in the community that contributed in no small measure to her being always on the move, seeking comfort, acceptance and affirmation outside the community. Eventually, before I came, she had made up her mind to leave for good in order to look for a place where she would have a sense of belonging and be cared for.

So, quite often we point accusing fingers at others; that 'this sister/brother is never at home', but we oftentimes never asked ourselves how our actions/inactions contributed towards his/her constant absence from the community, whether we show enough love, care and concern. We all need love and care. There is no need pretending that we are angels when we know that we are not. Holiness is born out of communal and not solitary lives. St Basil the Great in his Longer Rule, praised community living and demonstrated its advantages over solitary life. He singled out the mutual care and love that are characteristic of such a fraternal life together: Christ in his love for human beings, he said, was not content with teaching the word only, but practically demonstrated this love and humility by washing the feet of his disciples thereby teaching them by example to care for one another to the point of washing each other's feet. In Basil's words (RBas GA VII):[5]

> Whose feet then will you wash? For whom will you perform the duties of care? In comparison with whom shall you be (lower or even) the last, if you live by yourself? Yes, and the saying, A good and delightful thing it is when brothers dwell in unity, which the Holy Spirit compares to the high-priestly anointing flowing down from the head upon the beard (Psalms 132:1-2), how shall this be fulfilled through dwelling in solitude? For here is a kind of stadium for the contest, a good course on which to advance, a continual training, and a practising of the Lord's commandments – this is the dwelling together of brothers in unity (among themselves) (Psalms 132:1). Its goal is the glory of God.[6]

In mutually washing one another's feet, the living of the vows is made less heavy. For example in living out *our vow of poverty*, through it we learn to subordinate our desire for things to our need for people. We need people since we are not self-sufficient but are finite and limited in our capacities. We are human beings, who are in need of relationship with others, to care and be cared for, to value people and friends over the value of material things, to value being with our brothers/ sisters over having things. We need to use material goods not merely for our own survival but also in respectful interaction with others. The implication of our lives as social beings is that ultimately we are poor. This poverty has human growth through human relationship as its goal. Poverty on this level includes not only sharing of goods but also the sharing of what we have (knowledge, time, talents), sharing of what we are (life, values, dispositions, attitudes), and sharing of what we can (services, capacities, etc.). It springs from the truth that we are all insufficient and our completeness is only experienced in our relationship with others. Being aware of this fact will necessitate my finding satisfaction in my community. Also in a religious community where 'community life' works, each brother/sister will be provided for, with no individuals left to look outside for their needs. In the Acts of the Apostles we are told that distributions were made according to individual needs.

The *vow of chastity* is practised with greater security where a real sense of community flourishes in a genuine fraternal love that is reciprocated by all the members. One important contribution to the discussion of the vow of Chastity in the Decree *Perfectae Caritatis* is the stress laid on fraternal relations within a community. In traditional discussion on this vow, there is hardly a theme that receives greater attention than 'particular friendships'. But now we find the Council saying that Chastity has greater safeguards in a community where true fraternal love thrives among its members (PC 12).

The community can offer to each religious a selfless interest in his/her plans, a true concern, a sense of belonging, worth, solidarity and security. If there are failures in living the vow of chastity, particularly in friendships among fellow religious, the cause may in all likelihood be community living. There is the probability that what is effectively practised is common life and not community life. In a situation of this nature, it becomes pertinent to ask if we have supported and loved the erring brothers/sisters instead of criticizing, alienating, or competing with them. Do we try to 'suspecting the good' in our fellow brother/sister, instead of imagining what evil they do when they go out? The holistic understanding of chastity helps in no small measure in living out the vow of chastity: chastity of thought (thinking no evil), chastity of the heart (bearing no evil for anyone), chastity of the tongue (speaking no evil), chastity of the ears (not willing to listen to false accusations against anyone), and chastity of the eyes (not coveting, seeing no evil).

Many religious today desire and struggle for a meaningful experience of community. Community is both a gift to be valued and shared; it is a task to be done. To have a harmonious and joyful community life, each member must invest time and effort to create it. Religious are intended to be experts in *communion*, witnesses and architects of the plan for unity. Community life is a great support in being faithful to one's celibate commitment. To actualize the gift of self, we need affirmation from our fellow members. We need emotional support. Religious life is liveable only when we are assured of our community that is consistently supportive and loving.

Community is primarily for celibate loving. In celibacy we are meant to love one another and in this case, attitudes and dispositions are primary to our doing things, without which no poverty and chastity is possible. It is in *inter-action* that attitude gets deepened and it is in *inter-action* that my disposition gets pruned, empowered and chastised. It is in *inter-action* that life moves us into mature celibates. You don't become a celibate in yourself. It is in *inter-action* with other human beings that celibacy gets deepened and we get bonding depth: deepening and depth relationship. Community life when imbued with an affirming attitude provides the healthy social network that makes fidelity possible.

By the *vow of obedience*, the religious seek God through Jesus in their religious community and through its way of life. This however demands strong faith, and is supposedly the risk element in following the Lord. Faith, as we know is not just about prayer, contemplation, liturgy knowledge and wisdom. The faith which Christ's followers are asked to have is the biblical faith, which is about risk and relationship and trusting. A religious by his/her vows of Poverty, Chastity and Obedience should be aware that he/she has entrusted his/her life into God's hand through the community and should therefore know that each day is an adventure. A religious should be willing to take risks. Luke in his Gospel, as Fr Chris Thomas also pointed out, defines discipleship in terms of risking and trusting. Following Christ is about 'never being comfortable to remain where we are and about wanting more of God and of life. It's about pushing boundaries and living prophetic lifestyles.'[7] Obedience, for example, is a clear rejection of the image of the self as autonomous, solitary and disengaged. It is a declaration of our intention to discover who we are in the common life of the brethren, that is in a community. It is a commitment to be liberated from the unsustainable burden of the modern and lonely self.

4. Community Involvement: an Integral Aspect of Healthy Religious Life

To explain what I mean by community involvement being integral to healthy religious life, I would like to report an experience I had in Germany with a game which we played as a community.

On 24 October 2013 we went on an excursion to Vechta Jugendhof, a place for spiritual and moral orientation for Catholic youths. After meeting several of the people who work there we were asked to play a game as a community. In total we were sixteen nuns, all of whom were part of this game. The moderator of the game was a lady who worked at the institution.

This game aimed at the promotion of good 'group dynamics'[8] and required two groups and a moderator.

Group One: Four Sisters, who were 'blind' but mobile.

Group Two: The rest of the community who were able to see but immobile.

For the game, we were gathered in a big hall. The four sisters were told that they would be given a task to do and were sent out of the hall. In the meantime the rest of the community was asked to spread out to different parts of the hall. Some were seated down while others were standing. At a certain point the moderator told the community that everyone had to stop and remain where they were; they were to be freed by the four sisters who had been sent out.

In the meantime a circular space had been arranged in the middle of the room. Inside of this space was placed a hoop (forming a space within the space). We were told to imagine that the circular space was 'a lake' and that the hoop was an 'island' in the middle of the lake. On this island was a jar with medication inside. The players were told that they all needed this medication in order to be able to move again and that the blind sisters needed it to see again.

So at this point the common goal was to figure out how to get the medication off the island.

The moderator distributed one rubber ring (just

the right size to fit round the jar) and four long pieces of strings.

The players were told that the lake was full of acid so nothing should touch the water. She also ensured that the distance was too great for someone to jump across the water to the island to get the medicine.

Before the four blind sisters were led back to the hall, the moderator told the group that could not move to discuss a strategy and find out how to get the medicine out. Discussions and suggestions were coming from here and there from every member of the community. Eventually someone came up with an idea about how to get the medicine from the island which most agreed could work. There was a bit of skepticism but the moderator encouraged them to try it.

Meanwhile the four sisters who had been sent out were blindfolded and were told that they would be the ones to help in getting the medication off the island. That medication would bring wholeness to the community again. It would help those who could not move and it would also make the blind sisters see again. Once the others had settled on a strategy, the blind sisters were led back to the hall and were placed in four different corners. At this point the blind sisters began receiving instructions from the sisters who could see but were immobile.

The moderator had the task only of watching carefully what happened and interrupting if she saw that someone was in distress, afraid, muddled, or could not hear or understand the instructions which were coming from every quarter of the room, just like in a football match. The moderator did not give any solution, she only commented on the situation, pointing out where there was a difficulty, making the players aware of problems and asking how they wanted to solve those problems. The moderator gave the players positive feedback so as to strengthen their positive qualities.

So the group that could see but was immobile was telling the blind sisters what to do. They instructed them to look for the strings that were dispersed in the four corners of the hall. The sisters who happened to be standing next to one of the strings or the rubber ring automatically took responsibility (without being appointed!) for leading the blind sister nearest her to that object. When the rubber ring and each of the four strings had been obtained, the sisters were instructed to come together. It was agreed that they should congregate around Sr Carmen.[9] So they all started heading in her direction. The sisters who had previously been responsible for helping the blind sisters get the strings and or rubber ring, gave first instructions as to which direction to go in. However, for some, the distance was rather far. At that point, Sr Carmen was encouraged to say something so that the blind sisters had some sense as to where they should go. However, she did not do this, which made the task substantially more difficult. Eventually they did find their way to her and were instructed to tie the four strings around the rubber ring.

Other sisters who were further away, attempted to explain how to do this, but eventually it became clear that this was not useful, as those sisters were not in a position to see what needed to be done. Once again, Sr Carmen was requested to offer instructions, and this time she complied as best she could. The blind sisters were still somewhat confused, at which point Sr Austin, who was on the other side of the room but understood the task that needed to be accomplished, gave the sisters a picture of what they were to do: 'Imagine a compass,' she said. 'Each of you must tie your string to one of the four points of the compass.' This image enlightened the blind sisters and, with their hands, they were able to feel the four points of the compass and tie their strings to the rubber ring accordingly. Once accomplished, they were asked to go towards the lake. However, before doing this, Sr Austin gave a summary of what had already been accomplished and explained to the blind sisters the next stage of the mission.

After this, they moved ahead following every one's instruction with trust. Once again, without being instructed to do so, sisters close to where one of the sisters needed to be going, took responsibility for her getting there. So at this stage, rather than all four blind sisters listening to one of the others, each of them was being 'coached' by an individual in the special region where she needed to be going. A couple of times instructions were offered and the blind sisters asked for clarification. For instance, when the instruction was: 'Go left', a blind sister asked: 'My left or yours?' Three of the blind sisters were very careful to do precisely what they were instructed to do, no more and no less. Sometimes this required further instructions and more time than the instructing sisters expected. However, when those sisters were told to stop, they could be relied upon to stay where they were. The other blind sister was not quite so disciplined such that once she was positioned by the lake, she kept taking steps forward, drawing ever nearer to the 'acid-filled' water which she was, by no means, allowed to do. Therefore, even as the group moved on to the next set of instructions, it was necessary to continue encouraging this sister simply to stay where she was.

When they were well positioned at four different angles around the lake they were asked to bend down, each holding tightly to her string. Eventually most of the sisters felt that the four blind sisters were situated such that they could get hold of the medicine with the rubber ring. But one sister shouted from one end: 'No! Not yet, not yet.' She mentioned the name of one of the blind sisters and asked her to move a bit backwards so that the rubber ring could really fit in properly. When they did so, the sisters were able to drop the ring over the jar of medicine and pull it off the island over the lake.

Although this sister had previously only been responsible for instructing individual sisters who came into her vicinity, it was necessary for her to speak up at that stage to the whole group because only she, from her particular view point and from her unique perspective could see what nobody else saw. Those who were shouting: 'Good! Now draw the rope and pull up the jar with the medicine' were all right in a way because from their perspective the rubber band seemed to be situated perfectly. However from the other sister's perspective this was not the case which was why she was screaming: 'No! Not yet.' When the blind sisters did what that one person said, the whole thing became a big success and they were all whole again. The community was made whole again when the medicine was removed from the island.

Success! By Means of Good Group Dynamics

First of all, everyone, both the blind sisters and those who could not move, had a common aim which was for their common good. Everyone was aware of this goal and trusted that the others wanted to achieve it as much as they themselves did. This laid the groundwork for discussing which strategy to use. A variety of ideas were presented; some were considered carefully, others were practically ignored. However, the sisters did not defend their positions or try to gain support for them. In fact, once an idea was in the room, the sisters did not seem to think it was 'theirs' anymore, but rather one of the suggestions on the table. They kept in mind the common goal of getting the medicine off the island and were not motivated instead by the desire to be the one with the brilliant idea as to how to do it. It happened that Sr Carmen offered the suggestion which everyone agreed upon. However, as soon as it was decided, the plan was no longer 'Sr Carmen's' but rather that of the group.

Once the blind sisters came into the room, there was no need to delegate authority. Everyone understood that the next step was to attain the rubber ring and the strings, and those sisters standing closest to a given blind sister directed her to the nearest string (and the rubber ring).

The next step was not quite as easy because once it was agreed that the sisters should all move towards Sr Carmen, she stopped talking! This meant that the blind sisters could not easily find their way. (Although Sr Carmen had the bright idea to begin with, at this stage it did not even require a bright idea. She could have said anything at all – what was required from her was simply her voice, not instructions, yet she did not say a word.)

Even with this setback, the sisters did arrive where they needed to, and although some sisters had lost confidence in Sr Carmen at this stage, it did not matter; she was the one closest at hand and the only person in a suitable place to instruct the sisters as to how to tie the strings to the rope.[10] She did this to the best of her ability and, when it was clear that the sisters required more than she could offer, Sr Austin, who was far away and did not see the details of the situation but who understood in theory what needed to be done, spoke up, offering the blind sisters a 'vision': the picture of a compass. This enabled them to understand the bigger picture and to more efficiently and confidently perform the detailed task of blindly tying the strings to the rubber ring as Sr Carmen was instructing them to do.

At this stage in the game, once a first success had been achieved, the group breathed a sigh of relief and the sisters all patted each other on the back before advancing to the next stage. We also commended the blind sisters for how well they responded to the instructions given them and for the good questions they asked when something was unclear.

Before moving on, Sr Austin gave the blind sisters a recap of what they had already done and a synopsis of what they still needed to do. Then, as the blind sisters needed to go into four different corners again, the sisters closest to them once again took responsibility for instructing those individual sisters. Once again, they were not delegated to take on this role by the superior or the moderator. It was what made sense, and so they did it.

The final step was lowering the ring onto the jar of medicine at just the right angle. At this stage, once again the group had a variety of opinions but only one sister was situated such that she could offer precise and correct instructions

The Need to Broaden Perspectives for a Holistic Community Living

The group of players were thus able to arrive at a successful end because a variety of sisters took on different leadership roles when the situation called for that, and they were also prepared to step back and be quiet when that proved helpful. At the end, the blind group adhered to the view of one person who could, in that instance, see more clearly than the rest just as, at the beginning, the group adopted the strategy offered by one person, making it the group's strategy. In the same way Religious community could be a place of love, peace and joy if the brothers/sisters would adopt 'the broader perspective of 'me-and-you' instead of 'me-or-you".[11] One of the more readily quotable lines from Bernard Lonergan's *Method in Theology* is the following: 'Genuine objectivity is the fruit of authentic subjectivity. It is to be attained only by attaining authentic subjectivity.'[12] This authentic subjectivity is grounded precisely in these irreducible differences of subjective standpoint or individual perspective. True objectivity in other words consists in the awareness of the fact that there neither is nor ever will be a universal standpoint or perspective. All perspectives are by definition particular, so the authentic subjectivity which Bernard Lonergan meant or the broadening of perspective which is intended in this work does not mean overcoming the particularities of one's perspective or one's standpoint in order to embrace a communal viewpoint shared in common with other individuals – as we can see in the case of the game when the majority group said that the rubber ring was at the right position to get the medicine – but in getting more deeply in touch with the unique particularity of one's own subjective perspective in order to better appreciate both the similarities with and the differences from the perspective of the other individuals.

It is necessary at this point to explain clearly the subtle difference between standpoints and viewpoints.[13] Viewpoints are cumulative, so that by progressively walking around an object and looking at it from different angles one should be able to acquire a comprehensive or universal idea which takes in all dimensions of the object in question. Take for example the case of the medicine in the game. If all the sisters who could see had been able to go around the jar which contained the medicine, they would have had a comprehensive view which would have comprised all the dimensions of the object, in this case the jar. But standpoints, on the other hand, are fundamentally non-cumulative since they are grounded in the subjectivity of the viewer and not in his or her spatial location vis-à-vis an object. Human value judgments are the most obvious examples of standpoints, since, while claiming to be objective, they nevertheless bear the marks of the unique subjectivity, the individual life-experience, of the one making the value judgment. They are non-cumulative therefore, because they do not add up to a universal standpoint (as viewpoints add up to a universal viewpoint). To build up a holistic type of community both viewpoints and standpoints are necessary. Different standpoints can be quite enriching for community growth. For instance, every member in the community has a unique history, life experience, temperament and character all of which play roles in moulding, shaping and giving 'a special nuance' to the person's standpoint which no other person in the community will have.

5. *The Authority of a Superior*

The religious community which takes its origin from the communion that existed between Jesus and his apostles should also model its authority pattern on that of Jesus who in Mark 10:42-45 said that the Gentiles 'rule over' and 'exercise authority over' one another. These terms indicate *management* and *control*, but Jesus indicated that this style of leadership was not part of the Christian way of life. Elders were charged not to 'lord' or 'rule' but to 'become examples' to the flock (1 Peter 5:3). The real Christian method of leadership was not about *control* but about *service* (cf. Mark 10:44-45). As elders, shepherd (pastor) and overseer (bishop) of the congregation (cf. Acts 20:28;

1 Peter 5:1-4), they practise a method of leadership that is different from that in the πόλις (*polis,* 'city') and οίκος *(oikos,* 'family').[14] Authority or leadership roles in the New Testament involve becoming *examples, protecting and serving the congregation* (Acts 20:28, 35), *looking to the interests of others.* The Document on Fraternal Life in Community, *Congregavit nos in unum Christi amor (*FLC 49c), summarizing the role of the authority in the Scriptures says: 'Authority is, evangelically, always service.'

The Code of Canon Law, 608, says, 'A religious community is to live in a lawfully constituted house under the *authority* of a superior designated according to the norms of law.' Two important or essential elements that constitute a religious institute are *community* (meaning living together) and *authority* (in the person of a superior). The superior therefore is no mere coordinator, facilitator, or manager, administrator or moderator. He/she is all of these, but above all he/she has authority, meaning: the right under God, to tell those under him/her what to do. The superior is not merely someone who conveniently takes care of the needs of a group of people living together in an apartment. There is something beyond and above the role of a religious superior.

The Quadruple Authority Role of a Superior

When St Benedict says that subjects who listen to superiors are listening to Christ (cf. RB 5:4-6; Luke

10:16), he is using symbolic, quasi-sacramental language, which disregards the virtues, the human qualities or frailties of the superior. It is as if he is saying: 'Let them pay no attention to the person; the virtues, vices or other qualities of the one they obey, but only to our Lord Jesus Christ, for whose sake they obey.'

Besides this *sacramental* type of authority, there are others. The *juridical* type which defines the legal powers of the superior, for example, the power to delegate. The *organizational* type uses language which highlights his task of organizing the resources of the entity which he is serving, and the unity and implementation of decisions mentioned in FLC 50b-c are also under organizational capacity or quality. Finally, there is a fourth type. We refer to a superior as one who guides, calls, gathers together and challenges the communities and their members to promote the goals of the congregation, namely, the personal growth of its members and the salvation of souls. This is the role of a *spiritual authority* mentioned in the FLC 50a. This fourth type is called *agogical,* by Jan Hulshof because he said '*agoogos*' means 'guide'. He went on to say: 'as I attempt to figure out the idea of leadership, I do not think at first of the sacramental, juridical or organisational types of authority but of this *agogical* type. It refers to the superior in his role as spiritual guide.'[15]

It is not difficult to imagine the problems that

could arise from the combination of these different types of leadership – the *agogic* type (the superior as spiritual guide), the *sacramental* type (the superior as representative of Christ), the *organizational* type (the superior as an organizer of the community) and the *juridical* type (the superior as legal authority). This could lead to an abuse, given that superiors do not all possess the *charisms* of prudence and discretion to the same degree. However, religious authority is, in many fundamental ways, an important source of cohesion, stability, and continuity within religious communities. As the Document from the Institute of Consecrated Life and Societies of Apostolic Life, The Service of Authority and Obedience, *Faciem tuam Domine, requiram (*FT 1c) says: 'while *all* in the community are called to seek what is pleasing to the Lord and to obey Him, *some* are called … to exercise the particular task of being the sign of unity and the guide to the common search both personal and communitarian of carrying out the will of God. This is the service of authority.'

Authority 'represents' God, not that the Superior is humanly infallible in decisions. The superior's human limitations are explicitly recognized (cf. VC 92b; FT 13d, 18a, 21c, 25a), but authority should do its best in journeying with the members in the search for and accomplishing of God's will and in using methods sanctioned by the Church (the Word of God, the Rule of life and Constitutions, Chapter decisions, signs of the times, the studying of individual cases and so on). Authority is an indirect mediator (cf. FT 13c, 17c, 21c, 25). So whoever obeys, welcomes in a spirit of faith, by 'humbly submitting' to superiors, this mediation of grace which is offered and which gives a 'guarantee' that one is guided by the Spirit and sustained even in the midst of hardship (Acts 20:22-23 VC 92b). In the end, we are placing our trust in God who works through the community to which he has called us, and so we are placing our trust also in our brothers and sisters. This is a faith journey.

The 'Moderating' Role of a Superior in a Community

The game discussed above brings out very well another role of a Superior in a community as a moderator. A Superior is supposed to be a *moderator* and not always the speaker.[16] And in this game, the moderator even had an advantage which is rarely present in religious communities. She had moderated this game dozens of times and had a much better idea about what strategies could work or not work than the rest of the group. Even then, she did not force her ideas on anyone but rather encouraged the community to work together, to listen to one another and to remember the common goal. No matter how holy, knowledgeable or wise a Superior may be there is no way he/she would be able to see things clearly from every perspective. He/she sees things from his/her own perspective and that explains also why the wisdom of St Benedict made provisions for this perspective in his rule, though he spiritualized it by saying that 'The reason why we have said all should be called for counsel is that the Lord often reveals what is better to the young' (RB 3:3).

Again, a Superior is not there to solve problems but to comment and make the members of a community aware of difficulties which he/she sees and work together with them to find the best strategy for solving such a problem. The Superior should be one who is skilled in winning souls, who knows how and when to offer encouragement, how and when to kindly reprove by saying for example, 'Stop! Stop! Do you think this way you are going is the right way?' just like the moderator in the game.

For a Superior to be able to strengthen his/her team's dynamics he/she should be like the moderator in the game by using the following strategies:

A Superior has the daily privilege and responsibility of giving form to an unformed mass, and selflessness to people capable of selfishness. At the beginning of the game there was chaos but the moderator was able to give form and made the group to have confidence in themselves.

He/she should know his/her sisters/brothers: As a Superior and therefore a leader you need to guide the development of your community. He/she would start doing this by learning about the phases that a community goes through as it develops. When he/

she understands these, he/she will be able to pre-empt problems that could arise and call the community's attention to it before it happens. He/she should also know of the positive and negative roles that exist in any group situation and be able to reflect with the community on how these might be affecting them. This will help the Superior recognize potential problems before they arise or in their early phases, in such a way that the members of the community are part of the process. He/she should be aware that he/she is primarily an *administrator* and therefore his/her job is, in most cases, to organize and supervise.

He/she should tackle problems quickly with good feedback to the community: If as a Superior you perceive a potential problem or you notice that one sister/brother has adopted a behaviour that is affecting the reputation or the material good of the community, you should act quickly to challenge it, at the right moment and in a spirit of fraternal charity. You should do it in a way that it will be clear that you are fighting or defending the common good and not because your ego has been wounded.

He/she should define clearly roles and responsibility for each member in the community to prevent confusion. A Religious Order or community that lacks focus or proper direction can quickly develop poor dynamics as people struggle to understand their role in the group. In the above mentioned game the moderator was able to define roles at the very beginning of the game, making plain who was to do each task. The Superior of every community should make the rule or the Constitution of the order known to every individual Brother/Sister, for it is in this rule of life that the mission and objective of the Congregation/Order are stated and everyone's responsibility defined. Everyone should have a copy of the Constitution to be able to remind him/herself regularly.

He/she should pay careful attention in order to know when and where to come in, and watch how the community is progressing. A Superior should pay particular attention to frequent unanimous decisions, as these can be a bad signal of groupthink, bullying or group power grip. When such is the case in a community the superior could consider exploring new ways to encourage people to discuss their views or to share them anonymously. This is necessary because there are some people who are always afraid to air their views because of what the consequence could be but if they are sure that no one would know who says what then they feel free to express their views. What is important for the growth of any community does not depend on 'who' but on 'what' and 'how'. It is every Brother/Sister's responsibility to bring about this 'what' and 'how', and not only the superior's. It should be evident that the superior like a good moderator should make proper provisions for this to come about.

The superior has the responsibility also of moulding

a communal identity and helping people invest their lives and confidence in one another for the sake of a common dream and a shared mission. This was made tangible in the game and that was why the blind sisters were able to rely totally on the sisters with sight without fear of being misled. However, the Gospel and the constitution of the congregation provide continuous clues for demonstrating how people who are very different can be drawn together to appreciate, trust and co-operate with one another.

Establishing this togetherness in a religious community is not a small or quick task. Rather it is a continuous and sometimes arduous one. It is nonetheless noteworthy that superiors are uniquely positioned to help individuals relinquish their grip on personal preference. Superiors have the obligation to shape the community around the inspiration of Jesus, intentionally walking people into each other's lives, teaching them how to admire and appreciate fellow members who may often think and live quite differently. The motivation for this practice is clear: it is the belief that the love generated by a spiritually coherent community is greater than the sum total of the love emanating from its individual members' lives and it helps to foster fidelity to the vows as we have demonstrated above.

Leadership is mostly about identifying a vision and aligning a community with that vision, thus enabling the whole group to adapt. Leadership is systemic, social, and organic. A leader is not mainly out in front inspiring a vision. Rather, he/she is in the midst of congregational life, nurturing the process whereby genuinely adaptive change takes place, become nurtured and flower to maturity. Such a leader accompanies the community to the realization of their true identity, aim and goal.

Notes

1 George Guiver, Pursuing the Mystery, Worship and daily life as Presence of God, London 1996, p. 22.

2 Karl Rahner, 'Reflections on Obedience a basic Ignatian concept', pp. 371-372.

3 Jean Vanier, Community and growth, London 1979, p. 16.

4 Hence, a play of words; '*conspire*' from Latin word *con*: with, and *spire*: breath; breathing together.

5 The *Regula Basili (RBas),* is divided into two; the *Small Asketikon* (*RBas SM)* also called Shorter Rules or Shorter Responses and the *Great Asketikon (RBas GA),* called Longer Rules or Longer Responses. The *Small Asketikon* is the earliest stage of the composition of the *Great Asketikon.*

6 Anna M. Silvas, The *Asketikon* of St Basil the Great. (English translation of the Longer Responses and the Shorter Responses), Oxford University Press, 2005. p. 185-186.

7 Chris Thomas, 'Rediscover your first Love', in: *Good News, Catholic Charismatic Renewal Serving the Church*, No. 190, London July/August 2007, p. 28.

8 I borrowed this term from the social Psychologist Kurt Lewin who is credited with coining the term 'group dynamics' in 1947. He noted that people often take on distinct roles and behaviours when they work in a group. 'Group dynamics' describes the effects of these roles and behaviours on other group members and on the group as a whole. See Kurt LEWIN, 'Frontiers of Group Dynamics: Concept, method and reality in social science, social equilibria, and social change', in: *Human Relations*, 1,5-41, 1947. That is exactly why I decided to give that name to the game since we were not told what it is called.

9 The names used in this narration do not correspond to any real name they are forged names.

10 Sr Carmen's unwillingness to speak when she was asked to say something so that the blind sisters would with her voice detect where she was, did not make the community to condemn her and give her role to another sister. Instead they move on with her though some were no longer confident that she was going to be the same Carmen who brought up the first brilliant idea and eventually she later complied.

11 Helena Cornelius and Shoshana Faire, Everyone can win. How to Resolve Conflict, Australia 1996, p. 165.

12 Bernard Lonergan, Method in Theology, New York 1997, p. 292.

13 For a more detailed information read Robert P. SCHARLEMANN, The Being of God, New York 1981, pp. 31-38. He distinguishes very well standpoint from viewpoints.

14 Read Ron Clark, 'Family Management or Involvement? Paul's Use of προΐστημι in 1 Timothy 3 as a Requirement for Church Leadership' in: *Stone-Campbell Journal 9*, 2006, pp. 243-252, here p.249. Note; the word προΐστημι *(proïstëmi)* is a Greek word meaning 'manage' or 'rule'.

15 Jan Hulshof, 'Religious Superior and Spiritual Leadership', http://www.mariststudies.org/w/images/0/08/ 9FN_13_Hulshof_ Leadership.pdf pp.70-77, here p. 72.

16 Though in a monastic community, the Abbot/Abbess is more than a moderator. He/she is also a teacher (RB 2:11). He should direct his disciples with twofold teaching: words of mouth and by example of his/her life. He/she is expected to be the first to put into practice whatever he/she commands. Also the role of a religious Superior is more than being a moderator as we have demonstrated in the preceding paragraphs.

V

FINDING A RAISON D'ÊTRE OF RELIGIOUS LIFE

THERE HAVE BEEN immense changes in the last decades in the way religious life is seen and valued in the life and mission of the Church and in the society at large. These changes are perhaps signals for us to reconsider and to theologize anew out of our own experience the value, essence and the raison d'être of religious life in the Church. To do this we could ask ourselves first of all; what are the contributions that religious life makes to the richness of the ecclesial community. What are the distinctive roles of the Religious in the Body of Christ and what witness do the Religious give to the Church and to the world?

1. *The Ecclesial Community:* All Christ's Faithful

In the Letter of St Paul to the Ephesians he gave us a dynamic description of the ecclesial community as he says; each has been given his/her own share of grace, given as Christ allotted it, so that the saints together might make a unity in the work of service building up the Body of Christ, every joint adding its own strength, each separate joint working according to its function and so the body grows until it has built itself up in love (cf. Ephesians 4:7-16). With this Pauline text in mind we understand that a healthy ecclesial community would recognize and gives free play to these gifts that highlight, encourage and promote distinctiveness, all geared towards the growth of all. In such an ecclesial community there is equality of dignity and action and equality in commitment to mission yet there is uniqueness of roles. This reality finds its resonance in the Church's Code of Canon Law (Can 208) which says, 'from their rebirth in Christ, there exists among '*all the Christian faithful*' a true equality regarding dignity and action by which they all cooperate in the building up of the Body of Christ according to each one's own condition and function'. In another place the same Code says; The *'Christian faithful'* are those called to exercise the mission which God has entrusted to the Church to fulfil in the world, in accord with the condition proper to each (cf. Can 204 §1). Again it says '*All the Christian faithful*' have the duty and right to work so that the divine message of salvation more and more reaches all people in every age and in every land (cf. Can 211).

The four references above ought to speak to us religious in our attempt to articulate our unique role within the community of all Christian faithful. These passages, from the Scriptures and from the Church's Code of Canon Law, clearly preclude us from solving the question of our uniqueness in purely functional terms, as if our raison d'être must be found in what we do in the Church. We should be careful not to bear on our shoulders nor to appropriate to ourselves the primary responsibility of any aspect of the Church, because from the above texts we see that all aspects of the mission in the Church belong to '*all Christ's faithful*'. Then the issue should be to find out what lies at the heart of our own *charism*, if all the apostolic works which we have used as walls to safeguard ourselves are now falling apart and the Scriptures and the Church's law are telling us that they had never been our raison d'être, what then is the unique role of religious life in the Church?

In his apostolic exhortation *Redemptionis Donum,* 15, St John Paul II addressing the Religious said 'even though the many different apostolic works that you perform are extremely important, nevertheless the truly fundamental work of the apostolate remains always what (and at the same time who) you are in the Church'. In order to find out this 'what and at the same time who we are in the Church' I think we need to distinguish carefully between vocation to the religious life and the apostolate of the religious.

2. *The Religious Life and the Apostolate*

Before we can go into the relationship between the religious life and the apostolate it is necessary to know what is at the core of the apostolate of the religious. The apostolate of the religious is extremely diverse and they change with time, taking different shapes and forms in different countries and cultures. They incarnate in each congregation and in each Religious man or woman.

However, the apostolate of the religious can be generally described as: manifesting God's presence, goodness of life and witness; living for others; service – love in action; encountering the suffering humanity in the poor, the sick and less privileged; safeguarding and maintaining holy places and inviting and welcoming people to such places for pilgrimages and prayer. It is from this general mission that each religious order or congregation derives its contours and it is also from this that every single Religious man/woman takes up his/her own apostolate.

When we talk of mission or apostolate some people believe that the so-called 'contemplatives' have no mission, but that is a false assumption. Every religious order/congregation has received from the Lord a mission, be it an pre-eminently in proclaiming the

Word or in doing charitable work, be it a particularly internally lived apostolate like running a guest house all these are ways of proclaiming the same Lord bearing in mind that the fundamental work in all these is 'what and who we are' and this in real essence is total dedication and consecration of oneself to God in one's daily life.

In a world that puts much emphasis on success, achievements and usefulness, our concern for career, our eagerness to be useful tends to falsify what apostolate means and its real relationship with religious life. We are seduced into believing that our apostolate in terms of 'work' is what counts, we thereby lose sight of the essence of being a religious. We religious have specific tasks that we accomplish, but these tasks are not reasons for our existence as brothers/sisters. So we ought to exist even after these occupations and tasks have ceased to exist. Unfortunately, Religious life today has taken on the form of career institutions under the pretext of apostolate.

Religious life and apostolate are not mutually exclusive. In fact, our religious life might require us to pursue a certain profession. Many people have become excellent parish sisters/brothers, sister doctors and sister nurses in response to God's call heard in the community. Quite often, our vocation becomes visible in a specific job, in a specific task or specific apostolate. But our vocation as religious can never be reduced to these activities. As soon as we begin to think that our apostolate is our vocation then we are in danger of losing the whole sense of it all and religious life itself is devoid of any value. An apostolate disconnected from the religious vocation divides; but on the contrary an apostolate that expresses adherence to our religious vocation is the concrete way of making our unique talents available to the community. Therefore, it is not our apostolate, our tasks and our jobs but our religious vocation as brothers/sisters that should guide our lives.

Today we see before our very eyes the real experiential tearing-apart that so many active Religious suffer between seeking perfection and exercising their apostolate. It is too easy to say that this is all because of the overriding influence of modernism, secularism, materialism, and so on. It is significant that each religious Congregation, instead of blaming mankind for the present situation that demands her own modernization, looks inside herself for the reason and source of her reform. The real problem lies in knowing clearly the relationship and/or the difference between religious vocation and the religious apostolate. As Teilhard de Chardin says, what is difficult is not solving problems but formulating them, so having formulated this basic problem as religious, we have to be conscious of the fact that finding a way of solving it is of paramount importance because only in this way can we 'unify our up-to-now twofold contradictory activity; our religious life turning us away from the world and into ourselves and apostolic activity turning us outward to the world and its needs.'[1]

Edward Kelly went on to say that the religious has too long tried to live these two lives side by side, being victim to the debilitating tension this creates in him/her, rendering him/her largely ineffectual in both. We are neither authentically living the life of consecration nor are we genuinely 'there' for suffering humanity or even for that which we falsely take to be our apostolate; instead quite often we have been forced to find the answer to this intimate, pressing, personal problem in one of several ways that are not answers: 'to become all apostle and no Religious; to become all Religious and no apostle; or to continue uncomprehendingly dividing himself, giving now a little to God and now a little to the world — half-measures only making him an enigma to God, the world and himself.'[2]

The religious should only bear in mind that God has no need of his/her busy activity. What counts and what will always endure is that the one has acted in all things conformably to the will of God. Everyone is struggling and seeking all sorts of achievements and recognition. God obviously has no need of the products of our busy activities, since he is in himself sufficient. The only thing that concerns him, the only thing he desires intensely, is the faithful use of our freedom, and the preference we accord him over the things around us.

Quite often because of the busy activity in which

we engage in, we complain of stress but deep down our anxiety is a form of vanity, reassuring us that if we are busy, we are important. That makes us feel essential, more than mortal. The consequence of this is that we no longer have time for quiet moments with the Lord. We are too busy to recite our canonical prayers, too tired to pray and too stressed out to recollect ourselves for a moment, let alone find time to die, yet dying is what we are doing, from the moment we take our first breath. 'Scientists and physicians would agree with the German theologian Karl Rahner that 'we live a dying life.' But even as living consumes our energies, we forget about our dying.'[3] We learn to navigate by focusing not on 'what and who we are' but on our 'career', losing sight of our life and our being. That is to say that in our apostolate we should make the spirit of obedience and of union with God our sole concerns. If we find our work void of aim and purpose and therefore of no value in itself, we can love it for the opportunity it gives us in helping us grow in our faithfulness to God.

Apostolate: Witness of Love Expressed in Service

Essential to religious life is the desire to enter more fully into the pattern of Christ's life – a pattern of dying and rising, of self-emptying, and of allowing again and again for the transformed fullness of divine life to shape and ultimately become my reality. Just as in any kind of Christian vocation, the religious vocation is a call to surrender to Love and in this as in other forms of love, it sometimes seems foolish because it follows a different logic. Yet as Jesus said to his disciples: 'So with you: when you have done all you have been told to do, say, 'We are useless servants, we have done no more than our duty' (Luke 17:10).

Often we think of service as signifying a generosity and a giving over of one's talents, time, training, care and support for others – all of which can be true. But this sort of service can at the same time include a self-gratifying and a self-aggrandizing focus. A ready example of this can be seen in political life. We call our politicians 'public servants' and while politicians can do many good things for their constituents, they are often motivated by personal fame, enjoyment of power, and a desire to attain an even more prestigious position. Such ambition is very human and may not be wrong for people in the secular life, but all too often it is also present in those who serve in the Church. Although we can and should pray that God's grace can purify human ambition, if we do not also give selflessly we will run into the danger of not depending on God.

In religious life, a greater demand is made in terms of the quality of service. For the religious, whose identity is explicitly centered on Christ and on the radical pattern of his service, an essential element is the disinterestedness[4] of all that is done. Just as for Jesus there was no self-seeking or ambition in his preaching, in his miracles of healing, or in his arguments with Pharisees and Sadducees, so too are religious called to selflessness in the work they do.

The International Congress on Consecrated life held in Rome from 23–27 November 2004, took as its title 'Passion for Christ and Passion for Humanity'[5] and looked at the state of religious life through the lens of *Vita Consecrata,* and by means of two biblical images: the Samaritan Woman at the well and the Good Samaritan (cf. Luke 10:25-37; John 4:1-42). In these two passages *compassion* is the leading quality:

- The Samaritan woman met Jesus on her way (i.e. at the well), felt in her heart the fascination of the person of Jesus, of his mystery and of his message. She abandoned her old way of life represented in the abandoning of her jug, and was later transformed into a witness, an evangelizer and a *sower* of the Gospel (cf. John 4:5-42).
- The Good Samaritan met on his way another human being who was half-dead, a victim of theft and violence. His heart was moved to compassion for him and, interrupting his trip, he took care of him (cf. Luke 10:29-37).

When considering other passages in the New Testament from this perspective, one notices that the compassionate life is a life together and makes sense of the choice by the Congress to focus on this theme. Example of such passages are:

- Philippians 2:3-4; St Paul exhorts the Christians of Philippi to live a compassionate life with the mind of Christ, saying: 'Do nothing from selfish ambition or conceit, but in humility regard others better than yourselves. Let each of you look not to your own interests, but to the interests of others.'
- Colossians 3:12: St Paul stressed that the compassionate life is a life in community when he said: 'As God's chosen ones, holy and beloved, clothe yourselves with compassion ... Bear with one another, forgive each other...'

What St Paul makes plain is that *compassion* is not an individual character trait, a personal attitude, or a special talent, but a way of living together required by and going out from our life in Christ. Precisely, because we are so inclined to think in terms of individual greatness and personal heroism, it is important for us to carefully consider the fact that the compassionate life is community life. We witness God's compassionate presence in the world by the way we live and work together. Those who were first converted by the apostles revealed their conversion not by individual feats but by entering a new life in Community (cf. Acts 2:42-47).

The selfless service and compassion which ought to

characterize our lives as religious should be rendered first to our fellow brothers and sisters within our community. Strange as it may seem, what happens in our immediate communities is often ignored. We don't want to be of good service to the members of our community, instead we want to show compassion to people outside of our community, forgetting that charity begins at home. 'It can be easy to do inspiring things for the guests and visitors, easy to preach and to pray, but in the other members of the community with whom we live eyeball to eyeball we find the real test of the claim to be serving God. It can be relatively straightforward and satisfying to be of service to people at one remove from us, but community is an unfailing test of what all of that means. There, the things that we fail to be or to do are paid for by everybody else.'[6]

Compassion a Valuable Quality for the Apostolate

The International Congress of 2004 mentioned above singled out '*compassion*' or soreness of heart as a quality that could incite the religious to have passion for Christ and show *com-passion* for humanity. Jesus in Matthew demonstrates for certain that he had this disposition of heart in mind for his disciples, for he himself acted with compassion: 'And when he saw the crowds, he had *compassion* on them, because they were harassed and helpless, like sheep without a shepherd. Then he said to his disciples: 'The harvest is rich but the labourers are few, so ask the Lord of the harvest to send out labourers to his harvest' (Matthew 9:36-37). In this passage, Jesus is explicit about the demeanor with which he would like his labourers to go into his vineyard: Love and compassion ought to serve as an identity card of a religious life. And elsewhere he speaks out clearly against anyone who did not act in such a way. In Matthew 23:23 he admonished the Pharisees: 'Woe to you, teachers of the law and Pharisees, you hypocrites! You give a tenth of your spices – mint, dill and cumin. But you have neglected the more important matters of the law – justice, mercy and faithfulness. You should have practised the latter, without neglecting the former.' Far too often, it seems that people in religious life can be accused of the same thing. We give ourselves over to poverty, chastity and obedience but neglect the more important matters of the law; justice, mercy and faithfulness.

A closer look at the text of Matthew 9:36-37 considered above, will show us that Christ did not just have compassion but he had compassion because 'they were harassed and helpless, like sheep without a shepherd.' In other words, he had compassion because they were sinned-against.[7] By so doing, Jesus makes it clear that his call to evangelization, his call to religious or even priestly life is a call to *compassion* for the sinned-against. This is made clear by the fact that immediately after he had compassion on the crowd in the text above, he then says to his disciples: 'The harvest is rich but the labourers are few, so ask the Lord of the harvest to send labourers to his harvest.' So we are being sent into the harvest for the sinned against of the society.

In December 1984, St John Paul II, in his message of solidarity with all the poor people of the world enumerates different categories of sinned-againstness, especially as expressed in the actual forms of poverty: hunger, refugees and the unemployed, those who are alone because of sickness, old age or for any other reasons, the widows, the orphans, victims of physical or psychological violence, those who are deprived of their rights; rights to life, to freedom, to security and all kinds of marginalization.[8] This panorama of poverty or of sinned-againstness which strikes both the spiritual and the human values of a person in his/her dignity represents the objective of the preferential option for the poor. These are the areas where the religious is called to minister to the human misery and it is here that the heart of the religious apostolate lies.

If you scroll down the Gospel you will notice that Jesus always had compassion on the people, primarily because they were sinned-against. Let us have a quick look at some Gospel passages:

1. Matthew talks about Jesus going ashore and seeing a great crowd 'and he had *compassion* on them and healed their sick'.
2. And Jesus told his disciples to feed the people, ' I

have *compassion* on the crowd, because they have been with me now three days and have nothing to eat and I am unwilling to send them away hungry lest they faint on the way' (Matthew 14:14; 15:32).

3. Luke paints a similar picture. When the Lord saw a woman whose son had just died, he had *compassion* on her and said to her, 'Do not weep' (Luke 7:13).
4. And when the Samaritan saw the man beaten and wounded by robbers, 'he had *compassion,* and went to him and bound up his wounds… (Luke 10:33)
5. The parable of the Prodigal Son makes the same direct connection between *compassion* and the sinned against. Luke reports, 'But while he [the son] was yet at a distance, his father saw him and had *compassion* and ran and embraced him and kissed him' (Luke 15:20).

When we talk of ministering to the sinner and the sinned against, we can see and appreciate that these poor people are not necessarily the materially poor but often those who do not know the ways marked out for them by God, those who are not yet the adoptive sons/daughters of God, those who ignore the moral route that leads to true happiness. Therefore, the first work of this compassion which the religious is called to do is to proclaim in the light of the Gospel the truth of man created in the image and likeness of God. This is done not necessarily through preaching but by way of example; in being and doing. This can be done by a sister doctor, sister nurse, teacher, and so on, no matter what type of 'work' one is doing. The real apostolate work can be well integrated with the various career works or employment, which quite often we mistake to be our apostolate.

Sinned-against! By whom?

I can imagine what goes in people's minds when they hear about 'the sinned against'. One would immediately ask: by whom are they 'sinned-against'?[9] Answering this question from a biblical perspective one could reply, by principalities and powers of the world, by demonic forces which cast a bondage over human lives and human institutions or by witches and wizards. However, extending our mind broadly, we could also add, by the economic and political systems of our society. It is without doubt by all the above mentioned, but more precisely it is by other people with whom they spend their daily lives. We continually sin against one another through cheating, insincerity, double-dealings, calumny, detraction etc. All these canny ways we use to enrich ourselves, serve ourselves instead of serving Christ are the ways we sin against people, even though these people themselves might be sinners. Compassion for such people, brings the identity, vocation and mission of a religious 'back to its principal reference point rooted essentially upon the Gospel as a "foundational standard".'[10] The Gospel standard allows us to examine ourselves, to identify our individual different vocations in the common vocation which we share as religious and as Christians. The desire of every religious who really has passion for Christ should be to have love and compassion for humanity, for the world that has strayed, the poor and especially those who do not know God. Passion for Christ and his compassion for humanity are demonstrated well by the Samaritan traveller: when he came upon a *victim*, he overcame all his religious and cultural animosity for the Jews (cf. John 4:9).[11] He loved and cared for this *victim*. He bandaged the wounds, carried him on his own mount to the inn and had him looked after until he was well. He paid for his keep, and was even willing to take care of any extra expenses incurred. Thus he went beyond what the law required and what would be accepted as ordinary service to a stranger and performed a selfless and disinterested service. This is a heroic love and service given to a stranger. For me, it is here that the essence of Christian life is seen vividly: Showing heroic love, bringing the powerful love of God to people who were or who are your natural and political enemies and showing Christ's compassion to the less privileged, the sinned against in our midst.

Involvement: a Basic Element of Compassion

The greatest challenge in the religious life is feeling with and being close to the 'human drama', or rather, a full immersion in the condition of being human. Christ was not unconcerned about the suffering of the people of his own time, therefore religious called to imitate him should not be unconcerned either. It is necessary to face the challenges which realities present to us as religious and we should consider them as part of our identity as consecrated people. *Involvement* in the life of others is an inevitable aspect of consecrated life, *communio* and *missio* – and compassion born out of involvement bestows authority on our words, deeds and identity as religious. Take for example when John the Baptist sent his disciples to check on Jesus' messiahship, Jesus answered them: 'Go back and tell John what you hear and see: the blind see again, the lame walk … and the good news is proclaimed to the poor' (Luke 7:22; Matthew 11:4). Jesus based his authority not only on Isaiah's prophetic words in an abstract way but on his concretization of those words in his involvement with the poor and with the sinned-against of the society. In the same way a religious should base the authority of his/her mission on his/her involvement with the poor and should, to some extent at least, understand and live out the evangelical vow of poverty with the concrete living situation of those in need in mind and taking Christ as a model. It should be well noted that the poor here does not necessarily mean materially having nothing. We are all poor in different ways and we are deprived of our moral, spiritual and material rights every day. It is to these persons, stripped of their moral, spiritual or even material rights that we are called in the world to identify ourselves with in order to bring them back and give them strength.

To the sinner the Gospel implicitly says: Know your sinfulness, repent from it, bow in humility before God and receive forgiveness.

To the sinned-against in the same person, the Gospel says: Know that you have value, stand in defiance against the forces which deprive you of it and receive strength.[12]

In our Christian teachings when we encounter the word evangelism – missionary zeal or activity, we automatically think of people as sinners rebelling against God, needing repentance, and in response, receiving forgiveness. This is also correct, no doubt about that. But it is important to stress that people are not only sinners, they are also sinned-against. If a religious in his/her apostolate wants to proclaim the Gospel to the very depth of a person he/she must recognize and be conscious of the fact that the human person is both a subject and an object of sin and must address these two facts, otherwise no evangelism takes place.

If we are truly disciples of Jesus (2 Corinthians 4:5) and our service through Christ is to be redemptive, then we need to look to the quality of the interaction between us (the disciples of Jesus) and those to whom we render service (the sinned-against). In his apostolic exhortation, *Evangelii Gaudium,* Pope Francis implicitly says that in real life a shepherd always takes on the smell of the sheep, so *involvement* should be an imperative condition for one who has been called to deepen his/her baptismal consecration by means of the religious life. Thus the same apostolic exhortation (EG24) says: 'Let us try harder to take the first step and to become *involved.* Jesus washed the feet of his disciples. The Lord gets *involved* and he *involves* his own, as he kneels to wash their feet. He tells his disciples: 'You will be blessed if you do this' (John 13:17). An evangelizing community gets *involved* by word and deed in people's daily lives; it bridges distances, it is willing to abase itself if necessary, and it embraces human life, touching the suffering flesh of Christ in others. Evangelizers thus take on the 'smell of the sheep' and the sheep are willing to hear their voice.'[13] In this vein Fr Michael Casey talking about the power of this involvement or 'encounter' as he called it, says: 'For ministry to be revelatory of Christ's love there must be this personal encounter. In so many cases it is the human contact which is the most important element of the service rendered. Those who are experienced in nursing patients in intensive care know that touches and physical reassurance are essential in sustaining the spirits of those exposed to such a barrage of hi-tech medicine. The technology is important, but there are other factors that must not be neglected.'[14] In service the primacy of personal presence is never overstressed and this 'presence' is given in whatever form it is needed to the extent of 'smelling like the sheep'.

The service of Jesus was made possible only because of his human presence among men. Jesus' life and work were effective because of his solidarity with humankind; he shared the poor human condition. Religious cannot be separated from his/her fellow men and especially the poor. Compassion is possible only when we perceive people as our brothers and sisters who unfortunately are sinned against. If we look at them as sinners, we tend to criticize them, isolate them or, if we are good people, we may have concern for them or have pity on them, but can never have *compassion* for them. C*om-passion,* means suffering together with another, *cum* (with), *passione* (passion) having the same feeling with the person. No such shared feeling is really possible except on the basis of shared experience. To understand people as sinned-against we must see them at closer range. Furthermore, in the Gospel passages quoted, where Jesus had compassion, it was said: Jesus *saw* the people; Jesus *saw* a great crowd; the Lord *saw* the woman whose only son was about to be buried; the Good Samaritan *saw* the half dead man; the father *saw* the wayward son and had compassion and so on. So, we must be so near them as to *see* them and even to go so far as Jesus did – to feel their pulse and hear their sighs. We must be so near that these people become 'you' and not 'they'. As Raymond Fung puts it: 'They are those right in front of us, whose eyes we must look into, whose voice we cannot but hear, and whose very presence lays claim to our friendship. In short, we must be involved. This is the way we can come to understand people as the sinned against and the way we can begin to be compassionate.' [15] Compassion makes us other Christs to people we encounter and those who encounter us.

Religious Consecration and Apostolate: A Blend of Identity

In order to be able to enter into the life of the poor and live our lives as a 'memory of Christ's life' on earth, it is necessary that there be a real blend between the religious' identity of life and its apostolic ideal, that is, that type of work which we mysteriously achieve together or what is called *missio Dei*. There ought not be an opposition between service and dedication.

The mission of the religious by so doing acquires all its ecclesial dimension and therefore is able to open itself to the totality of the suffering humanity. The work of compassion, both spiritual and corporal, constitutes the field where the love of God is exercised in its fullness. Just as there is no limit to human misery, which extends and grows in its diverse manifestations, so also there is no limit to the apostolic activity and love of the neighbour. Every human privation, every suffering, every necessity demands attention, relief, consolation, light, solidarity and in a word, love.

Essentially, we are inseparably religious and apostles: our vocation is not at all a juxtaposition of the separate and distinctive vocations, because the apostolic action and the love of the neighbour together form the very nature of our religious life. If we could remember the origin of our religious vocations we would remember also that when we felt called to the religious life, we did not make the decision in two different phases: first the choice for the consecrated life and then the option for a determined apostolate. For me religious life was and is presented in a concrete form. Most candidates who opt for this or the other religious order have little or no knowledge of the difference between the congregations. Some were just attracted either by the religious habit or they visited someone and were struck by the way they pray or by the way they live together and do things together. In the same way if there is an indissoluble and intimate union between the religious ideal and the apostolic ideal, it then follows that neither of the two can be absorbed by the other. The religious offered in holocaust the availability of his/her life and is freed from any impediment in order to love and to live always near the Lord and to consecrate him/herself closely to Him. This total self-donation by means of the three vows is made manifest in the religious apostolate which is a concrete way to show or to prove his/her love of God in his/her institute.[16]

However, it should be emphasized that this *missio* or the apostolic ideal that we are talking about here should not be mistaken for an activity, performed through our charismatic zeal, or through our expertise as teachers, doctors, nurses nor with the 'work' which we are currently involved (that is to say the apostolate of each congregation). The *missio* about which we are talking in this work is the grace bestowed upon us with each other to share the *Missio Dei* and *Missio inter gentes. Missio* taken in this sense is the reason for our existence as religious. We are co-sharers in the mission of the Holy Spirit who is sent by the Father through the Son.[17]

The theological and spiritual dynamism of this *missio* is what we find in the Gospel figure of Jesus. The apostolic mission of Jesus cannot be reduced just to his preaching and healing activity. His entire life of witnessing love and service is part of his apostolate. This witness reaches its highest degree in the hour of his supreme sacrifice on behalf of humanity. Jesus is the apostle-martyr of love towards the Father and for humanity. To this effect, *Vita Consecrata* says: 'The task of devoting themselves wholly to 'mission' is therefore included in their call; indeed … consecrated life becomes mission, as was the whole of Jesus' life' (VC 72a). 'The more consecrated persons allow themselves to be conformed to Christ, the more Christ is made present and active in the world for the salvation of all' (VC 72b).

The variety of the mystery of Christ, the Apostle of the Father, is the foundation of the different apostolic *charisms* in the Church. Since a single institute cannot embrace nor exhaust all the richness of that mystery, it is shared among different religious congregations. For example, some specifically witness 'the mysterious apostolic fruitfulness' of Christ (VC 8b), some the 'praying' Christ (VC 8a; 14c; 24b; 32d), others are dedicated to alleviating human suffering, thereby offering an outstanding witness to Christ the 'divine Samaritan' (VC 83b) who in his ministry of compassion revealed the merciful love of the Father to the suffering humanity, others are the living presence of Christ the Teacher (cf. VC 96a; 97a) and so on. This many-faced mystery of Christ is what is called the apostolate. As Timothy Radcliffe puts it: 'to be an apostle is to have a life, not a job … The apostolic life is therefore for us more than the various apostolate that we do. It is a way of life.'[18]

The delicate identity of a religious

Religious life is both precious and precarious, a tenuous matter of heartbeat and breath. The image I usually use to describe it is the image of an egg (chicken egg). If you hold an egg in your hands you have to be extremely careful how you hold it: neither too tight nor too loose. If you hold it too tight you may end up breaking it, but on the other hand if you do not hold it tight enough you can end up letting it fall and be smashed. So is our religious vocation: If we hold too much unto the fact that we are called to be the memory of Christ's life on earth as the Apostle of the Father, we can become arrogant about it all, considering ourselves as being the spiritual elites, making people believe that we enjoy a special connection with God. The danger of this way of thinking is that it divides the people of God into 'ordinary' and 'special' Christians, with the result that the religious-apostolic ideals no longer lead to togetherness but to separation.

Besides, if we lose the real value of religious life such that it be confused with 'career life' then we have stopped existing even if we still parade ourselves as religious. This is unfortunately the danger we are running into today, and that also is partially one of the reasons why we don't see again the importance of our lives as religious. We are running the risk of losing our identity as religious; what is left for us is either the name 'we are religious' or the habit for those of us who still wear them. Otherwise we are left with a tiny pectoral cross.

3. The Unique Role of Religious Life

We have tried to bring out the inherent nature of religious life and the apostolate, however, it must be said that 'a religious life, which would simply be a witness of the Gospel in the world, is something that has lost all its specific character. After all, a good social worker, a good nurse, a good teacher who witnesses to the Gospel in his milieu does not have to be a religious to do that.'[19] This means that we must expect something entirely different from the religious, what is distinctive in the vocation to the religious life.

The uniqueness or distinctiveness of the religious life lies in its eschatological nature, i.e. the witness to values beyond their temporal and spatial realization in this world. Distinctive lifestyles in the Church are complimentary to each other; while for example the non-religious laypeople bear witness that God is to be loved *in omnibus* (in all things), religious witness that He is also to be loved *super omnia* (above all things).

- Religious are to remind their fellow pilgrims of the goal of their journey, to point to the transcendent. This they do, not primarily by what they do in terms of apostolate but by being a sign, a sacrament of the mystery within the material world. The notion of sacramentality is inextricably linked with their eschatological witness.
- Religious are to be a 'splendid sign in the Church' (Can 573), their 'magnificent vocation in the Church' (RD 2) is 'to foretell heavenly glory' (Can 573). They are a sign of the world to come, a sign of the Church's mystery (Can 607).
- Religious are to be, in their whole being, a living memory, a continual reminder, hence also the

importance of a religious habit which is an external sign of their pointing to something. They are not only to keep the memory alive but also active and operative.

- Their sacramentality is linked to the sacramentality of the Eucharist and the command of Christ 'Do this in memory of me'. At the Last Supper, while instituting the sacrament of his Body and Blood, Jesus confirmed the announcements of his redeeming death and gave to the apostles the memorial of his sacrifice and said to them: 'Do this in memory of me' (Luke 22:19; 1 Corinthians 11:24-25). In an analogous way, at the beginning of his public life, Jesus called the Apostles to a life of special following. Accepting his invitation, they left everything and followed him. Forming them with his examples and teachings to live with and like him, He handed on to them his way of being and acting, his 'way of life', implicitly saying: 'live this way in memory of me'. So what the religious do with their lives is in memory of Him. This indeed is the fundamental service they render to the Church. Thus *Vita Consecrata* says: *'By virtue of their identity, consecrated persons constitute a 'living memory of Jesus' way of living and acting* as the Incarnate Word in relation to the Father and in relation to the brethren' (VC 22). The apostles transmitted, therefore, also through their exemplary life the unchallengeable heritage received, the '*apostolica vivendi forma*' (VC 93c; 94a).

- The Religious should be 'voices' that affirm with confidence and conviction; 'We have seen the Lord. He is risen. We have heard His Word' (EE 35).[20] We are to accomplish and signify the entire purpose of the whole economy of redemption, for it is in this mystery that we recognize our 'identity' and 'dignity' (RD 16). It is 'the profound sign of this mystery that each of us bears within him/herself' (RD 15).

Eschatological Witness

In the Church and in the world it is all too easy to lapse into a matter-of-factness without depth or mystery, but the religious, 'fixing their own life and vocation ever more firmly within mystery' (RD 1), are to be anchor for the ecclesial community, keeping it located in the Mystery.[21] They stand with their fellow pilgrims primarily and forcefully as those who live as if they could see the invisible (cf. Hebrews 11:27). This call of religious to give an eschatological witness or to be an eschatological sign of the Kingdom has two dimension; the incarnational and the transcendental. These are intertwined and one needs the eyes of faith to see the transcendental in the embodiment of the realities of our Christian faith.

- In the incarnational dimension; it is clear that

the religious whose life and essence is totally to announce the transcendent, announce it as immanent.

- Then in the transcendental dimension; the religious who is him/herself immanent, takes the religious dimension of reality seriously and commits him/herself to his/her daily human activities. By their very existence they proclaim to the world that religion is not optional and that all earthly realities are incomplete without it. Sr Helen Lombard captured the synthetic meaning of this reality when she says: 'the mystery of Christ pondered, remembered, embraced, celebrated, lived, brings all earthly reality to be savoured according to its true nature. There is a striking synthesis of the secular and the sacred in the very person of the consecrated religious. This synthesis parallels the integration of faith and culture, faith and life.'[22] These are the ultimate justification for the existence of mission or religious apostolate.

The very life of the religious is an indication to the ecclesial community that following Christ does not spring from an acceptance of a certain system of ethics, the ethics of the vows for example, but from a personal 'yes' to a personal call, 'from the interior encounter with the love of Christ, which is a redeeming love' and which 'embraces the whole person in that person's unique and unrepeatable personal "I".' (RD 3). In this light, one understands better the expression that St Benedict took from St Cyprian and that is summarized in his Rule (4:21) – the monks' programme of life: *Nihil amori Christi praeponere*, 'Prefer nothing to the love of Christ'. The eschatological witness of the religious consists in this valid proposal for the sake of love. The religious surrenders all things and counts them as nothing if only he/she can possess Christ (cf. Philippians 3:8). So the religious life is a 'sign' that by its mere presence evangelizes.

Eschatological Sign and Prophet of the Kingdom

Religious are representatives of the Church as the Bride of Christ in her final glory at the end of time. Their vow of Chastity is bound up with the mystery of the covenant of love between Christ and His Church. Not only does it establish a unique personal relationship with Christ, but it is a foreshadowing and anticipation of the fullness of redemption. It is a sign of eschatological fulfilment, pointing the way for mankind's advance. Our existence as religious is like a signpost pointing to the Kingdom. Thus Fr Timothy Radcliffe was said to have one day asked an especially lazy brother what he was doing. The brother replied that he was being an 'eschatological sign', waiting for the kingdom.[23] We are analogically useless in the eyes of the materialistic mind because the real value of our life is eschatological. The mere fact of being there as religious is already a value of its own. The value of religious life is inherent in the life itself. That's why the apostolic exhortation *Vita Consecrata* says that religious life is a prophetic life, prophetic of the Kingdom.

Religious Life a 'Prophetic Life', are we Prophets?

This expression 'Religious life is a prophetic life', in my view can be likened to its twin expression 'Religious life is a life of perfection'. Both expressions can be very presumptuous if they are left so piously vague. We have tried to explain the latter affirmation in the first chapter of this work. Now, we come to the second expression; 'prophetic life'. The only way such an assertion would have meaning is when it is the life form, and not the individual religious, that is characterized as 'prophetic' – the religious life-form is a prophetic life-form.

Just as entrance into a religious community (the word religious meaning devout, pious, reverent, godly etc.) does not mean that one is religious and therefore godly, there are many genuine, devout godly people who do not enter religious life. So also entering religious life does not make one a prophet and there are many prophetic figures who do not enter religious life. However, different life forms in the Church offer corporate witness to particular dimensions of Christian life in which all the baptized are called to participate.[24] All are called to be religious, in the sense of being godly, to fidelity, to fruitfulness and to prophetic witness. But certain life forms, such as religious life, matrimonial life, or lay organizations raise one or another of these dimensions to particular visibility by their corporate living of this *charism*. So what follows makes no claims that all the religious are prophets or that religious life has any monopoly on the *charism* of prophecy in the Church.[25] Instead, the religious life-form as corporate witness to the *charism* of prophecy should explicitly challenge its individual members to the exercise of this *charism* and empower, support, and promote their fidelity to this *charism*. The felt call to prophetic ministry and the gifts of spirit, mind, and heart for the exercise of such ministry, therefore, should be among the factors in discerning a vocation to religious life.

Moreover, the value of religious life as a life of perfection; that is also an eschatological sign of the transitoriness of life and a prophetic life form is multidimensional in roles that are in turn distinctive and inherent to it. Such qualities or dimensions can be summed up by saying that:

- The value of religious life is being witness of the spiritual life and to manifest its splendour and its value.
- Religious life is an expansion of the Eucharistic life.
- The role of the layman, woman or the role of any baptized Christian is to imbue the family, first

of all, with the spirit of the Gospel, hence the creation of the Christian family is an admirable role. Again, their task is to render present the spirit of the Gospel in professional life, in the economic society of our time. The baptized Christian also is supposed to give presence to the spirit of the Gospel in political life, i.e. to have some of the spirit of Jesus Christ pass over into the organisation of the city of man.[26] So, the religious should not take on his/her shoulder such a role, for theirs is a very distinctive role: precisely to bring out in relief the specific character of the spiritual life.

- The role of the religious is made manifest in a precise way by its transcendence what the life of the spirit represents.
- Religious life should be a contradiction to that which the world calls value. The authenticity of such a life is not displayed in the type of apostolate specifically but rather in the type of life lived. So, some of those apostolate which were being done by the religious in the past and are being now taken over by the lay ministers have never been the essence of religious life. Therefore, religious ought not cease to exist just because those duties are no longer reserved for them.
- The religious life is not a sort of inferior level of the priesthood; accomplishing the secondary tasks, which the priests would give them, e.g. giving out Holy Communion to the faithful or to the sick,

washing and ironing vestments; albs and soutanes. It is good if the religious in any way can render such services to priests but this should not be the end of the religious life.

- The essential purpose of the religious life is to witness to the fecundity of the grace of Christ and of the grace communicated by the sacraments.
- A religious, by the fact of being a religious, is a daily, continual, living preparation for the coming of Christ into the lives of others.

Finally, it should be noted that the religious, in the words of Karl Rahner 'are *in* the world the expression, the visibility, the representation of a quite definite peculiarity of essence in the Church, namely her world-transcending origin and destiny. Hence they must be in the Church as the historical visibility of the world-transcending and eschatological grace of Christ, and they establish, therefore, *in* the Church as such, a special class (station) so that this differentiates its occupant theologically and not only canonically (Can 491 §1: *religiosi praecedunt laicis*) from Church-people in general, and hence from the layman.'[27]

Eschatological Witness Demands a Distinctive Stance Towards Earthly Reality

The religious through their response in faith for a distinctive vocation in the Church 'have made a paradigm shift. They have drawn new boundaries round reality. They proclaim a new meaning-system. They see life differently. They have taken a different stance.'[28] This distinctiveness which is also located in the 'extra quality' of life demands a distinctive stance towards an authenticity of action, hence the kind of significant action that is authentic for a religious might not be authentic for a non-religious. We cannot authentically live within one paradigm yet act out another if our religious witness is to speak with authority. There should be consistency between our private and public action otherwise we face the danger of privatizing religious life not to mention hypocrisy! Instead we should be conscious of the fact that the totality of religious consecration requires a witness to be given publicly, by the whole life, so that this becomes a public proclamation of the absoluteness of the Kingdom (EE 32-37). By doing so publicly, we also make ourselves answerable to the outsiders that is to say as Sr Anneliese Herzig puts it, anyone is then free to ask me: how is it then with your vows? I have therefore made my life available that it could be subjected to criticism.[29]

The religious should learn to unify his/her life. The temptation is for many religious to live in a series of parallel lives. This is no problem for business people, for professionals and politicians who keep separate their professional life from their family life or their professional life from their religious practices. For religious this is a contradiction in terms; for all activity forms part of the life, the jobs are done as being done by a brother/sister/priest. Otherwise, the central element of the person's being is lacking; simplicity, which consists in having one single goal, one single preoccupation in life and this is what St Paul was saying in 1 Corinthians 7:34; when he gives instructions to the unmarried about 'having a divided interest'. That's why it itches the ears to listen to many religious who have lost sense of what their lives are all about. They see themselves as medical doctors, teachers, nurses, professors, doctorate holders and so on, forgetting the basic thing and the only thing they are: priests, brothers or sisters. That, for them is no longer relevant, it is rather their professional expertise or their apostolate that give them identity. Little wonder why the world collapses when such apostolate ceases to exist or when they are no longer, either for reason of ill-health or old age, able to exercise such job the person dies a psychological death.

If we are really sacramental witnesses, the efficacy of our lives as 'sign' will have a radical challenge of some elements in our cultures and there will be no question of us being carried by the waves of the society. Philip Murnion, in addressing the subject of the future of a sacramental Church writes:

> I am arguing that the choices we make of the way to link private belief and public action will be critical and will seriously affect the quality and power of

> our sacramental witness … I am convinced that our society badly needs the kind of re-shaping of its ways of thinking and acting that can be nourished by the presence within of a committed sacramental community … My fear is that just as we come to appreciate more fully how much a sacramental approach to life is necessary for addressing today's social problems, we may be allowing the very sacramental quality of our own life to slip away from us.[30]

The sacramental witness which we are in the Church and to the world, is also a call to give a counter-cultural witness to the society, and this is a powerful witness. For we must challenge with the Gospel and with our lives the symbols within our culture and not just let ourselves be swept away with the cultural wave. Again as Sr Helen Lombard noted: this challenge of cultural values can be effectively done not in words alone but ultimately through one's whole *conversatio,* a lifestyle that proclaims 'the Kingdom is at hand … For clarity of sign and therefore power of proclamation, there must be congruence between identity and the way identity proclaims itself in life-style and in all levels of significant action.'[31] Our terms of engagement in the world must always witness to a radical level of disengagement. They must sacramentally express the distinctive stance to reality that we have taken, a stance inherent in our identity as religious. This engagement we have in the world should protect, promote and highlight our distinctiveness, so as not to violate the intrinsic dynamic of the kind of people we are. Our aim should be to engage in the world of work in a way which is an authentic expression of personal identity. There is a great danger that we might become too much absorbed in some cultural issues that, by our life commitment, we have chosen not to be absorbed in, that of course diminishes the capacity and the quality of our witness.

Eschatological Witness Demands Hope

Religious are dedicated to an eschatological existence as preference and emphasis, but not as an exclusive concern. Besides, religious today are not absolved from temporal concerns, from making their contribution to human development and the building of the earth. They can engage in the same works as the laity, such as teaching, hospital assistance, social work, any human endeavour; only that their approach to such engagements will be different. They come to human tasks with an eschatological eye to the future, to what is not yet, to what will come in the final age, but already begun in Christ. In this sense they live in hope. No matter how important the classes they teach, the hospital they work or their social involvement, they bring to their work in the world a sense of the *Deus semper major*, 'the greatness of God' of the person of Christ who is to be revealed in the Parousia[32] and therefore must be loved *super omnia,* 'above all'. Religious life, in other words, is a human value as well as an otherworldly one. It is important today to see religious life under this double aspect. It was born as a countercultural reality, and one criteria of its fidelity to the mission is precisely that of maintaining itself as an alternative meaning.

The religious have the commitment to become a channel of the Spirit in the works and actions of daily life. This commitment gives them a sense of purpose, a kind of quiet determination to persevere in their calling freed from a mere competitiveness or the pressure to be successful in secular terms only. Because whether they succeed or fail, they know that they are infinitely valuable in the eyes of God. In this light they discover that no moment escapes the possibility of divine inspiration and guidance, even the most mundane. They believe that all that has been and will be is enough reason for thanks because in the end everything that comes from God is a good and perfect gift. Hence the famous words of that great man, Dag Hammarskjold, 'For all that has been … thank you. For all that will be … yes.'[33] That is the witness of religious life, the eschatological witness of hope for the afterlife.

This witness to hope also applies to our very lives. We may feel that our own lives are rapidly going nowhere. But we can only be a sign of hope for a generation that is living through a crisis if we are able to confront our crises with joy and serenity. It can be part of our vocation as religious to confront crises in our vocation as moments of grace and new life. Fr Timothy Radcliffe reminds us to remember in every Eucharist the crisis of Maundy Thursday night. Jesus, he said:

> could have run away from that crisis, but he did not. He embraced it and made it fruitful. So, if we encounter a moment when we can see no way ahead, and when we may feel tempted to pack and go, then this is precisely the moment when our religious lives may be about to ripen and mature. Like Jesus at the Last Supper, this is the moment to embrace what is happening, and trust that it will bear fruit. That is part of how our vocation witnesses to hope.[34]

Religious are not 'strangers to their fellow men or useless citizens of the earthly city' (LG 46). On the contrary they embrace the world in its truth and reality. They see it as inchoate glory, as the Kingdom of God in embryo, and yet as 'no lasting city,' as a moment in an evolutionary process, and as less than the ultimate Good that is Christ reappearing and handing the Kingdom over to His Father. In a word they live in hope, and this hope is the secret of the joy that must be their witness if it is to be true. For them as for the married people joy is the surest guide that they are living their vocation in Christ hence the

Letter of Pope Francis to the Consecrated men and women; 'I want to say one word to you and this word is joy. Wherever consecrated people are, there is always joy!' This joy is a sign of hope for those whose life is eschatological. For the religious who is undergoing a moment of crisis, for couples whose marriage is going through a difficult time. Then our joy faced with uncertainty should be a sign of hope that every human life is on the way, God has not finished with us.

Notes

1 Edward Kelly C.S.S.P., 'The Religious Life and the Apostolate', in: *AFER* 7, No 3 1965, pp. 215-219. Here p. 215.

2 Edward Kelly C.S.S.P., 'The Religious Life and the Apostolate', p. 215.

3 Kathleen Norris, 'Everyday Mysteries: A Religious Life in the Real World', in: *The Mennonite Quarterly Review* 82, 2008, pp. 7-12, here p. 8.

4 Note, 'disinterestedness' is here used not as to mean uninterested but unbiased by personal interest or advantage or not influenced by selfish motives.

5 Passion for Christ Passion for Humanity. Acts of the Congress on Consecrated Life, Pauline Publication, Nairobi, 2006.

6 George Guiver CR, Pursuing the Mystery, Worship and daily life as Presence of God, London 1996, p.21.

7 In order to understand the appropriateness of the phrase 'sinned-against' in this context and in the subsequent paragraphs we need to digress a bit to throw more light on the sinned-against and the sinner/sinning. Let us examine by way of example the Shakespeare quotes: 'More sinned against than sinning'
Lear:
Close pent-up guilts,
Rive your concealing continents and cry
These dreadful summoners grace. I am a man
More sinn'd against than sinning. *(King Lear Act 3, scene 2, 57-60)*). See 'The Tragedy of King Lear', in: *Poetry and the Drama. Shakespeare's Tragedies*. Everyman's Library, Edited by Ernest

Rhys, London, 1910. P.613-614. Thrown out of doors by his own daughters, the anguished king Lear cries upon the storming heavens to execute justice, since he is now powerless to do so. Having ceded his authority, and been betrayed for it, the king comes to realize that he is but 'a poor, infirm, weak, and despised old man' *(line 20)*. As the storm beats down on his naked head, he invokes the 'dreadful summoners'—the gods who tend to judgment and retribution—but hastily adds that he is himself 'More sinn'd against than sinning.' In this pathetic moment, Lear exemplifies in the extreme a possessive parent with ungrateful children, as he chalks up their transgressions on a cosmic balance sheet. He has done wrong sometimes (what with all the 'sinning') but not as much wrong as his daughters have done to him (the 'sinned-against' part).

What made king Lear a sinned against was that he has become; powerless, poor, infirm, weak, a despised old man, coupled with the fact that he did not receive a fair treatment from his children. Important to note also, is the fact that, king Lear was both a sinner and a sinned against.

8 L'Osservatore Romano, 26-27 Dicembre 1984.

9 Quite often the temptation for the religious is to associate themselves closely with the rich and the affluent people of the society either for their own personal enrichment, i.e., because of the support which they are likely to receive from them or because it is not all that demanding a task to convince them of the Gospel. Fung Raymond observed two different reactions of people with regard to the Gospel message.

'A gospel that does not address people as the sinned-against poses no problem for those who do not feel that they are the sinned against— mainly people in the upper brackets of society, people who benefit from the social, economic, and political system. Sinned-against-ness is not part of their experience. And so, looking at themselves, they can honestly say, 'We have become Christians because of hearing the gospel, and the same has made us prosper. What can be wrong with it?' They do not acknowledge that they are the sinned against, or for that matter, that anyone else is the sinned against'. *'A gospel that does not address people as the sinned against poses a lot of problems for those who are the sinned against*—mainly the poor. There are often two kinds of responses from the poor to the gospel—outright rejection or accepting the fate of the sinned against as something outside the bearing of the gospel. In the first case, no evangelism takes place; in the second, religion serves as an

opiate'. Raymond FUNG, 'Compassion for the sinned-against', in: *Theology Today*, 37 No 2 1980, p. 162- 169, here p. 163.

10 Passion for Christ, Passion for humanity, p. 12.

11 In the above cited Scriptural passages it is very clear that none of the people having compassion cared to know why the misfortune had fallen on the victims; was it because of their sins or what? In the case of the Good Samaritan, he did not care to know whether the man beaten by robbers was a sinner, or whether it was because of his sins that he was beaten. No, he was interested in the sinned-againstness of the victim.

12 Cf. Raymond FUNG, 'Compassion for the sinned-against', p. 162.

13 The stresses on the italics are mine.

14 Michael CASEY, 'Compassion: The Mainspring of Ministry', in:*Tjurunga* 38, 1990. Pp.3-12, here p.6.

15 Raymond FUNG, 'Compassion for the Sinned-against', P. 165.

16 Read Jean Jérome HAMER, OP, 'Il Senso Ecclesiale della vita Religiosa al Servizio dell'uomo dell'America Latina', in: *SCRIS* 11, 1985, pp. 57-64.

17 Cf. José Cristo Rey Garcia PAREDES, ‚Die Hoffnung als unsere Sendung im europäischen Kontext' (Fortsetzung), in: *OK Ordens Korrespondenz. Zeitschrift für Fragen des Ordenslebens* 51 (2010), pp. 452-469, here p. 457.

18 Timothy Radcliffe, Sing a New Song, p. 124.

19 Jean DANIELOU, Nuns, What is special about them? London 1974, p. 5.

20 A document of the Sacred Congregation for Religious and for Secular Institutes, *Essential Elements in The Church's Teaching on Religious Life,* St Paul Editions, Boston 1983. Further references in the text will be cited as (EE).

21 Read Helen LOMBARD, 'The Distinctive Role of Religious', in: *Tjurunga An Australasian Benedictine Review*, 28 1985, pp. 3-13, here p. 8.

22 Helen Lombard, 'The Distinctive Role of Religious', p. 8.

23 See Timothy Radcliffe, Sing a New Song, p. 217

24 The word 'corporate' is here used as in 'organic,' not as in 'corporation'.

25 Based on Sandra SCHNEIDERS, 'Task of those who choose Prophetic Life style'; the fourth part of a five-part essay on the

Meaning of Religious Life Today, in: *National Catholic Reporter. The Independent News Source,* Jan 7 2010.

26 See Jean DANIELOU, Nuns, What is special about them?, pp. 4-8.

27 Karl RAHNER, 'The Lay Apostolate', in: *Cross Currents* 7 No 3 1957, p. 227.

28 Helen LOMBARD, 'The Distinctive Role of Religious', p. 9.

29 See Anneliese HERZIG, In der Spur Jesu. Leben nach den Evangelischen Räten, Innsbruck-Wien, 2012, p. 27.

30 Philip MURNION, 'A Sacramental Church in the Modern World', in: *Origins, N.C. Documentary Service* 14 (6), 1984, p. 87, 90, 84.

31 Helen LOMBARD, 'The Distinctive Role of Religious', p. 11.

32 The term "Parousia" is a transliteration of the Greek word παρουσία. In classical Greek the word meant "presence" or "arrival." The Greek word Parousia here corresponded to the Latin word *adventus*. After the biblical period, the doctrine came to be known as the Coming (*adventus*) or the Second Coming of Christ. So here it means the re-appearing of Christ on the last day.

33 Cited by Timothy RADCLIFFE, The Future of Religious Life, in: C21 Resources, Boston College 2011, p. 6-7, here p. 6.

34 Timothy RADCLIFFE, The Future of Religious Life, in: C21 Resources, Boston College 2011, p. 6-7, here p. 6.

VI

THE PLACE OF ORATIO IN THE FOUR PILLARS OF RELIGIOUS LIFE

RELIGIOUS LIFE IS a 'special' way of Christian life (LG 44; PC 1), because it is the way of the evangelical counsels institutionalized in the Church. The evangelical counsels, which are 'manifold' (LG 42) and meant for all Christians, are reduced in this case to the three values of chastity, poverty, and obedience. These counsels can be lived independently of religious life (LG 42) or concretized in an approved institute in the Church (LG 43). In the latter case they identify the religious life.

The Church's Code of Canon Law has a single thread that links these four principal factors or rather the four pillars of religious life. It is 'God's call' (cf. Can

574 §2). This call is a challenging fourfold invitation:

- to love God above all, seeking ever closer union with him – *oratio*
- to publicly profess the evangelical counsels – *consecratio*
- to serve the Lord of life apostolically – *missio*, and
- to be with others in a specific ecclesial community – *communio*

In order to place *oratio* in its proper place and give a sense of inner unity to the four pillars, we turn first to the call. Thus the call originates in God, who loves and consecrates the person called. Consecration makes us persons who are given to God without conditions. More concretely, it makes us 'living memories of Jesus' way of being and acting' (VC 22) of his obedience, poverty and chastity. It transforms us into signs and communicators of God's love for humanity. God's love evokes the generous total response of the person consecrated by him: it makes such a response possible. Not content to be merely 'dead to sin' by baptism (cf. Romans 6:11) 'but also renouncing the world,' the religious seek through the public profession of the evangelical counsels to 'live for God alone' *Perfectae Caritatis,* 5. Their vows are three aspects of a single 'yes' to God, giving expression to a basic acceptance of his loving proposal. God's grace-filled offer, once accepted, liberates the called person to love God totally and to serve him, as and where need arises, as an active member of the religious institute within which vows are taken.

From biblical and theological point of view, religious life is a 'special' form of life, the existence of which corresponds to the 'design of the Lord Jesus' (VC 31a), who was always docile to the Father (VC 22b). It is one of the various lifestyles in which ecclesial life is lived, by the will of the Holy Spirit, because 'diversity is also a work of the Spirit' (VC 31b). This lifestyle, therefore, has its own peculiar identity. It must be first of all a living presence of Christ in the world: 'The consecrated life truly constitutes a living memorial of Jesus' way of living and acting as the Incarnate Word' (VC 22c). This is the most characteristic note, both among Christians and non-Christians. Consequently, the consecrated persons, have the task of making present even among non-Christians (cf. LG 46; EN[1] 69) the Christ who is chaste, poor, obedient, (*consecratio*), Christ who is prayerful (*oratio*), Christ who is a missionary, hence sent by the Father (*missio*) and Christ who lived in communion with the Father, gathering disciples around him (*communio*). This idea is captured in the following diagram:

The Consecrated Life

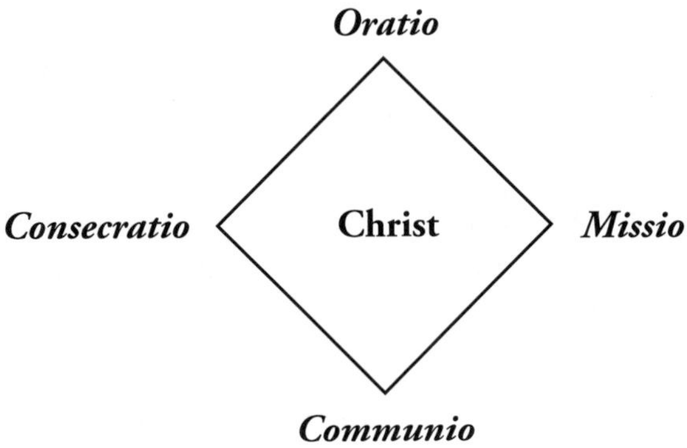

The quadrilateral image above illustrates the four pillars of religious life. The purpose of this is to have a visual image of how these four principal factors interact with each other and how they are built. It is not for the purpose of pitting one of the factors against the others; for example to pit *oratio* against *missio*. The lines of the quadrilateral are all equal. Their equality is necessary to create the diamond-shaped square. The exterior angles represent the four principal and interconnected factors of religious life. The supremacy of *oratio* over the others is evident in the image and it is an obvious statement that should not need to be underlined. However, that does not in any way belittle the importance and the essential role of the other three. The position of *communio* in the diagram is also worth noticing and commenting on: *Communio* (community) is at the base of all the other three. It is situated at a specified place as the centre of operations. It is the pedestal, the foundation of the pillars, because we are better apostles precisely thanks to our community, and not in spite of it. Community reminds its members that they have to take care of their personal journey of faith in the clamour of apostolic life (*consecratio*). So community life will be that stubborn insistence from which the call will be heard to safeguard moments of contemplation/prayer in daily life (*oratio*). It also represents that insistence which, opportunely or inopportunely, at moments of direct confrontation with diaries full of apostolic appointments, calls the religious to spaces in which he/she dares to share his/her own experience of faith. Community helps its members to relativize the pressure and importance of their apostolic tasks (*missio*).

Jesus came to give us God and his love. This is God's good news! So a religious who is not first and foremost giving God to humanity, which is the great hope that we can offer, our first prophecy (*missio*); whose style of life is not countercultural to a world centred on efficiency and production, on economy and well-being and is not presenting him/herself as a sign of God's grace and love (*consecratio*); who is not struggling to break down barriers between individuals in order to live harmoniously with the brothers/sisters (*communio*); who is without a deep personal relationship with the Lord (*oratio*); such a religious is a 'religious dummy', for the person is just a mannequin used in displaying religious life and not real. Consequently when any of the above factors is missing, you have something else but not religious life.

Religious life is said to be reinvigorated when the four pillars are harmoniously employed. Thus vitality is identified with such expressions as: impassioned following of Christ, radical discipleship, evangelical radicalness, witnessing to the primacy of God, evangelical spirituality, intense prayer, apostolic dynamism, missionary enthusiasm, lively communities, simple and open communities, option for the poor, and intense fervour. All these are accomplished through a vital and deep relationship with the Lord whom we wish to follow with a lifestyle and mission to which we are wholeheartedly full-time dedicated by virtue of our religious consecration. This 'offering' will be possible, authentic and fruitful only if it comes from a profound evangelical spirituality that helps people to mature in all the dimensions of their lives; a strong spirituality, incarnated, committed, nourished with the Eucharist, prayer, communitarian life, like a true school of holiness, flowing into a profoundly mystical experience that is contemplative both in daily life and in the mission.

1. Christ at the Centre of the Four Pillars

The presence of Christ at the centre of the diagram is indicative that first and above all, the religious should put Christ at the centre of their existence. The fundamental norm of our life is 'the following of Christ set forth in the Gospels' (PC 2). The consecrated life essentially consists in personal adherence to Jesus as our first and exclusive love; hence our commitment to live the vow or promise of chastity. Seeking Christ constantly, seeking his Face, and setting him at the heart of our lives, so as to be transformed into 'a living memorial of Jesus' way of living' (VC 22). Pope Francis admonishing the religious says, 'Like the Apostle Paul, let yourselves be captivated by him. Let yourselves be touched by his hand, led by his voice, sustained by his grace.'[2] Then he went on: 'Once again, we have to ask ourselves: Isaiah Jesus really our first and only love, as we promised he would be when we professed our vows? Only if he is, will we be empowered to love, in truth and mercy every person who crosses our path. For we will have learned from Jesus the meaning and practice of love. We will be able to love because we have his own heart.'[3]

The Second Vatican II Council in *Perfectae Caritatis* says that 'the members of each institute, therefore, ought to seek God before all else, and solely; they should join contemplation, by which they cleave to God by mind and heart, to apostolic love, by which they endeavour to be associated with the work of redemption and to spread the kingdom of God' (PC 5). So without cleaving to God in Christ neither the community life nor the apostolic service would be a success. The fuel to sustain this sort of life comes from Christ himself, as we encounter him in prayer, in other people, in the Eucharist, in the Scriptures and in the events of our daily lives. It is the same Christ who 'emptied' himself in order to assume our full humanity with all its weaknesses (cf. Philippians 2:6-8). This 'emptying' was for our sake, that he might more fully identify with us so that we could identify with him. To be Christ-like is to be compassionate.[4] Being compassionate means to enter into the deep wounded heart of the world. This means to identify with the poor, the sick, the imprisoned, the homeless, the dying, the exploited, the oppressed and all the sinned-against of our society, all whom God identifies with. However, when we open ourselves to the hurts and pains of the world, we inevitably open ourselves to our own hurts and pains as well. Too often, we have experienced brokenness in our own lives and are in need of the transforming embrace of God. Once we have reached this point, we are at the threshold of action. One step of action could be to begin to avoid our own hurts and pains by avoiding the hurts and pains of others. The other step of action allows God to transform our pain by using us to heal the pain of others.

Subsequently, in and through *oratio*, *consecratio,*

missio and *communio*, we enter into union with the divine Word, Christ. Meaning that we also enter into the hurts and pains of others. We often read that we are to be like Christ. To be like Christ is to embrace the brokenness of our world. This is the Christ who was born in a stable, died between two thieves, and rose from the dead out of a stranger's tomb. Thus the Cross is the very epitome of His self-revelation. God is not revealed in divine power and glory, but in human disgrace, poverty, suffering and death. The Cross of Christ is the epicentre of Christian faith and self-understanding (1 Corinthians 2:2), the core of Christian theology, its key and its foundation, the content of Christian preaching and the source of energy for the religious.

For this reason, when we look closely at the quadrilateral image of the four pillars, we can notice that it has a hidden image of the cross at the middle which embraces all the directions. The vertical beam reaches from the lowest depth of *communio* (humanity – humus – clay) through Christ who is at the centre to the highest zenith of *oratio* (divinity – God). The horizontal beam stretches to the breadth of the world, which is from the individual person's *consecratio* (self-giving) of him/herself to God in Christ to the breadth of apostolic services of *missio* (hence the words of Jesus 'Go ye to the whole world proclaim the Good News' (Matthew 16:15). This means that there is a cruciform structure to every one of the four pillars. In this sense, the Cross is not an external object that belongs far away to a hill in Jerusalem. Rather the shape of the cross is internal to the religious and to the Christian life in general. When we look at the different conflicts in the religious life and in our individual lives, we find that they are places where two intimate but conflicting realities criss-cross. Beyond and above all the criss-crossing of the religious challenging fourfold calling (*consecratio, missio, oratio* and *communio*), the presence of Christ at the centre is an assurance that we shall 'never be called to walk the lonely path of suffering without seeing the footprints ahead of us which lead eventually over the brow of the hill where Resurrection awaits us.'[5] If the Cross is the eyepiece, the Resurrection is the telescopic lens. We cannot understand the Cross without the Resurrection and the Resurrection presupposes the Cross.

So the cross is one's daily life, and it is present wherever Christians endeavour to be an Easter people. The self-denial of religious, therefore, will be the self-renunciations inherent in being all things to all men (1 Corinthians 9:19-23), in fostering community, in giving generously in the apostolate. As a disposition for religious/Christian life, discipline and *ascesis* are necessary. Today, this discipline would better consist in the cultivation of the openness, understanding, welcome, and patience that are the necessary framework in which charity can operate rather than in the corporal penances and often meaningless gestures of some religious rules. Love is all that is needed for the cross.

2. Oratio *as primus inter pares among the Four Pillars of Religious Life*

Though the four pillars of religious life are all of equal necessity for an institution to be a religious institute proper, yet prayer is *primus inter pares* (first among equals). Personal relationship with God in Jesus Christ is the only condition for the success of the other three. Little wonder, the identity crisis and role confusion which submerged and besieged religious life today.

The primacy of prayer in the life of religious is clearly brought out in *Perfectae Caritatis* 5 and 8. PC 5 encourages the members of each community to combine *contemplation* with *apostolic love*. By the former they adhere to God in mind and heart and by the latter they strive to associate themselves with the work of redemption and to spread the Kingdom of God. It is interesting to point out that the document uses the word 'contemplation', which shows that both the so-called active apostolate religious as well as the contemplative religious are also called to contemplative life.[6] Going further, the document PC 8 said that the religious call to follow Christ (*consecratio*) and their service of him (*missio*) must have its source in intimate union with him (*oratio* or *contemplatio*).

Thus *oratio* serves as the *primary* component of religious and Christian life. It is the foundation and centerpiece for the other three principal factors. Prayer support is imperative for green-lighting any issue. Without it, the remaining three are irrelevant. Therefore, the four principal factors in the Quadrilateral (the diamond-shaped square) are not equally weighted. Though they are equal components, *essential* and *necessary* in determining what religious life is all about, yet *oratio* (prayer) could more adequately be described as playing a unilateral role within the trilateral constituents of *communio*, *missio* and *consecratio*. However, for an institute to be a religious institute or for an individual to be a consecrated religious, prayer alone is not enough. One who has 'prayer' and is not consecrated through the vows, nor lives in a community, and does not engage in any apostolate, that is one who has no *communio*, no *missio* and no *consecratio*, this person could be taken to be a devout and pious Christian but not a consecrated religious. The same is true of any of the other three factors. That is why we said that they are all equally essential and necessary components of religious life but the weight they carry or the role they play are hierarchical.

Moreover, we can see this quadrilateral means of viewing the four principal components of religious life, with *oratio* as its pre-eminent centre but interfaced with *communio*, *missio* and *consecratio* as dynamic and interactive aids in the authentic answering of our call to following Christ in the religious life. Such a method takes it for granted that the *oratio* here in question fundamentally means 'personal relationship with God in Jesus Christ', a relationship which is a result of or a re-action to an antecedent action of God who has long initiated this journey of relationship with the soul and is therefore waiting for response. Understood in this sense, prayer therefore is not a mere attending of Mass, Liturgical Hours, reciting the Rosary, Adoration, etc., but a deep rooted relationship of love with Jesus by means of all the above activities. In a word, it means 'living prayer'.

This fourfold method of viewing the theology of religious life could be more fruitful for contemporary theologizing in their effort to decipher the essence of religious life. It preserves the primacy of Prayer, which profits from the spiritual and moral support of the brethren in the community, while accepting the discipline of a selfless service in the religious apostolate. When all harmoniously blend together, the consecrated sister/brother then becomes sacred in the sense of *consecrare, consecratio,* to make sacred. In such a quaternity, *oratio* is clearly unique. But this in turn is illuminated by the collective role of *consecratio, missio* and *communio*.

3. Oratio *as an intrinsic and ultimate value in religious life*

It is not heartening to notice what is happening in religious and priestly life today; the organic unity of prayer-community and consecration-apostolate is terribly threatened by imbalance. Today the pendulum has swung from an excessive 'verticalism' and the individualism of a Jesus-and-me piety to human, social, and secular preoccupations. Religious life has become so horizontalized, and the prayer aspect seems to have suffered in the change. Religious not only seem to be praying less, though perhaps giving more into activism in the name of apostolate, some even question the very possibility of a direct, personal encounter with God or intimacy with Christ in prayer or *contemplatio*. Theocentric spirituality in the religious life is giving way to anthropocentric Christian life, one that is person-centered, community-centered, and world-centered. Sad to say, this new trend is not even the real community spirit which is also an essential part of religious life but a socializing in the sense of common life without any moral or spiritual commitment. Slogans, such as 'find God in other people' or 'my work is my prayer' are at the opposite end of the spectrum of what Vatican II in *Sacrosanctum Concilium* (SC) said about the liturgy as the *culmen et fons*, 'source and summit' of Christian life. This is true of prayer in general; it can be paraphrased by saying that *oratio est culmen et fons* of the Christian life. Prayer in general in its sense of both: liturgical communal and private prayers are all sources and summit of our existence as consecrated men and women. Moreover, there are some religious who deceive themselves by saying that prayer and charity for neighbour is all prayer and so there is no problem. This attitude is dangerous because just as prayer which does not reach out to God in people becomes insincere prayer, so also action which is not consciously informed from within by prayer becomes insincere or untrue action.

Today in most religious houses, the chapel is deserted and human involvement canonized in the name of the apostolate. The spectre of activism and the heresy of good works may be detected in some of what is passing for apostolic love. Originally, religious communities were structured for a life of prayer and the apostolate was a consequence. Today religious communities want to be immediately apostolic, to be outgoing, comparatively unstructured and amorphous, and in so doing are giving in so much to activism. Except for daily Mass, a limited Office and perhaps some few common prayers, the trend is to leave the prayer life up to the individual religious. There is no intention of minimizing prayer, only the reducing of the quantity of prayers. A visit to some religious apostolic communities strikes one to reflect and question oneself anew what could possibly be the rightful place of community and prayer in the life of a religious. Isaiah this type of life viable and effective as a life consecrated to God and to his service? Unfortunately many religious who are living in such an atmosphere are used to this shapeless form of religious life, so much so that it no longer strikes them that something is basically missing in such a way of living religious life. Prayer ought to be the necessary (*fons et culmen)* support of the apostolate and not the fruit of an apostolic life.

4. Communio, *the Matrix of Prayer*

In the Christian family of God and in religious family, community (*communio)* is the ancillary of prayer (*oratio)*. In other words, the community is the matrix out of which authentic prayer is developed because there we find Christ in his different forms. This is to say that we should begin with life, with being Christians, men for others, men dedicated to breaking down barriers and creating community, and let prayer evolve out of this human effort. Prayer in the first instance is the celebration of community in Christ and only in the second instance and by a reverse action the source and nourishment of the apostolate. Christian life has always been circular, a rhythmic, ever-ascending spiral that moves between reflection and action, prayer and apostolate.

Each person finds himself in the *koinonia*, as every person comes to live through interpersonal relationships; he also finds Christ there. This is one of the challenging new perspectives of Vatican II (PC 15; LG 44), to see community as the place of encounter with Christ. Too often we have seen community as an obligation, as bringing Christ where He was not present before. This is also a valid idea, because we are bearers of Christ's love. But it is only one side of the picture; we also go to community to meet Christ. The entrée to prayer is community. The ability to contact Him depends on our ability to know and love our brothers/sisters, to gather together in His name. Prayer is nothing other than the explication and celebration of this Christian vocation.

Our lives are thus one life in Christ, a search for Him who lives on in His members. The transcendent God is immanent in the fellowship of Christ. The Christian does not have two lives, one a life with God and the other with his fellow man. He lives at the point of intersection of the divine and the human, the vertical and horizontal, the upward and the outward thrust. Love of God is love of neighbour, and love of neighbour the love of God, precisely because Christ, the Incarnate Word who identifies Himself with people, is the centre of our lives.

If our lives are really in Christ we shall want to celebrate this fact. The liturgy represents this fact. It acknowledges the Paschal Mystery being worked out historically in our midst. It reminds us of our history, of God's saving action in the past. It proclaims what is to be when Christ will have achieved His full stature in His people and God will be all in all. We celebrate the liturgy, moreover, with signs and symbols of daily life, to integrate chapel, classroom, nursing or marketplace, to give unity and integration to the multiple interests and concerns of our daily existence. The liturgy must also be a vital one that comes out of our lives and expresses what we are endeavouring to do. It is mystery, but the mystery must be expressed meaningfully. The centre of the liturgy is Christ, but the whole Christ, Head and members, and by our participation we express our faith that He is also the centre of life itself. The celebration is communal, because community is our life.

Prayer is an ultimate value, unquestionably the ultimate value of religious life, however apostolic the congregation. The answer to the objection, therefore, must go deeper. It must recall the fact that genuine community terminates in Christ Himself and fairly cries out to celebrate this fact in prayer and therefore community is celebrated in the liturgy. A religious community that is too preoccupied with its works to take time out to celebrate the liturgy together; religious who are too busy to make room for reflection and explicit encounter with Christ and the Father would make one question whether or not Christ is the centre of their lives. If they are united only in function or for efficiency, then there is no need for them to celebrate their community of love or the authority of Christ in their midst. But if Christ is their inspiration, then, however busy they are, they will know that prayer is the pearl of great price in their lives. Prayer will serve to put them on guard against self-deception. It will purify their love for one another, inspire the forgetting of self and generous giving. But these are its functional, lesser roles. Above all prayer will be the explicit assertion of what the apostolate and Christian life is all about, namely, 'the excelling knowledge of Jesus Christ' for which we have suffered 'the loss of all things' (Philippians 3:8-9).

So the success of a religious community (*Communio*) and its apostolate (*Missio*) chiefly depends on prayer, hence PC 8 said that for the members to answer their call to 'follow' and 'serve' Christ, their apostolic activity *must need to* have its source in intimate union with Him. This prayer which is the privileged expression of the love of God, the vertical dimension of Christian existence, guarantees and sustains the Community's fraternal love, the horizontal dimension. To know in a practical way the potentiality of prayer in the life of the individual religious and in the Christian community at large, there is need for a proper investigation into prayer: What is prayer, how does one pray in spirit and in truth, what are the characteristics of prayer? Such questions might go a long way to help us discover that union with Christ is likewise communion, *koinonia*, with other members of Christ. This is the reason why Christian prayer in and through Christ, is communal by its very nature. Even in the most intimate, private prayer the Christian cannot disassociate him/herself from his/her brothers/sisters; they are part of him/her and he/she takes them wherever he/she goes. Thus Christian prayer always has the dimension of community, either explicitly, as in the liturgy, or implicitly, as in private prayer.

Bringing this chapter six to a concluding point we have to insist that there is inner unity in these four principal factors of religious life. Religious are primarily apostles by what they are and not by what they do. Their apostolate 'consists mainly in the witness of their consecrated life' (Can 673). What counts most is not what religious do but what they are as persons consecrated to the Lord (Pope John Paul II).[7] Through their vowed life religious affirm that God is to be supremely loved. Their vows are apostolic in the sense that they state that earthly life is of value in so far as it is imbued by heavenly goods already present, and that essentially this life is a pilgrimage towards the glory of the heavenly kingdom (LG 44). An austere life of prayer and penance further strengthens the witness of consecrated persons (Can 673), 'prophetically' raising questions about values that human culture takes too much for granted. Apostolic action which has its roots in the call is always to proceed from intimate union with God (PC 8; Can 675 § 2). In so far as it is a loving response to God's call, involving service and death to self, apostolic activity will confirm and foster union with God (Can 675 § 2). Therefore there is an interaction between prayer and apostolic activity. Union with God is the soul of apostolic activity, and in turn service of God present in the brethren is a fresh input for prayer.

The whole life of the religious is to be imbued with an apostolic spirit and the whole of their apostolic action animated by a religious spirit (PC 8; Can 675 § 1). The lifestyle of the institute will take into account that it exists to reach out apostolically. On the other hand, the apostolate is clearly to bear the imprint of consecrated persons who publicly profess the evangelical counsels and joyfully live the fraternal life in common. Thus the life of a religious should be characterized by a thoroughgoing interpenetration of apostolic activity, prophetic values of religious life and a firm personal relationship with God in Jesus Christ. The consciousness of the members will be clearly marked by both the apostolic spirit and by religious spirit. These are to be lived out wholly within the ecclesial community which mediates God's presence and holiness. The special pact of consecration of religious is lived out within the community of the institute, which is the ground upon which the Holy One is loved and served.

Notes

1 *Evangelii Nuntiandi* (1975).

2 Pope Francis, Video-Message for the Vigil of Prayer at St Mary Major on the Occasion of the Opening of the Year of Consecrated Life (29 November 2014).

3 Pope Francis, Apostolic Letter to All Consecrated Persons on the Occasion of the Year of Consecrated Life (21 November 2014), 1:2.

4 There are three linguistic expressions of compassion that underline what it means to be compassionate. The Latin root words literally describe compassion as 'suffering together with

another'. The Greek root words literally describe compassion as 'a wrenching of one's guts'. The Hebrew root words literally describe compassion as 'a powerful emotion of birth that yields personal and societal transformation.'

5 John O'DONOHUE, Eternal Echoes. Exploring our Hunger to Belong. London, 1998, pp.172. John O'Donohue was an Irish poet, author, priest, and Hegelian philosopher. He was a native Irish speaker, and as an author is best known for popularizing Celtic spirituality. He died in 2008.

6 The English word 'contemplation' carries quite a lot of baggage with it, and is often misunderstood. We tend to think of contemplation as something done by the so-called 'contemplatives', which would be good reasoning, but for the fact that common usage tends to restrict the term 'contemplative' to men and women living a monastic life. But contemplation is not the exclusive preserve of monks and mystics. It is the Christian call to an intimate union with Christ.

7 St Pope John Paul II, Message to the plenary session of the Sacred Congregation for Religious and Secular Institutes (March 1980).

CONCLUSION

THIS WORK HAS been an attempt to highlight some essential and fundamental aspects of the religious life, with the hope that certain clarifications have been made on the identity and essence of religious life which have been in a state of debilitation in these last decades.

It started with a sketchy overview of history in which the theological identity of religious life with its fundamental basis in the religious identity of Christ was brought out. The historical survey has helped us to clarify and thus understand the role of the Holy Spirit who animated men and women to model their lives on that of Jesus, following the examples of the Apostles.

We have been able to see that the earthly life of Jesus was marked by the fact that:

- He was *consecrated* by the Father (John 10:36).
- He was sent out on a *mission* (John 17:18-19).

- In order to carry out this mission for which he was sent he needed energy and power from above, and therefore he withdrew quite often to *pray* (Luke 5:16).
- He called his Apostles to a life of communion with him and their response led to the formation of a *community* around him (Mark 3:14).

So Jesus' religious identity is based on four inseparable elements: *Consecratio*, *Missio*, *Oratio* and *Communio.* Religious life inherited from the Apostles these four elements as its foundation pillars. These four realities are intertwined and exist in, with and for each other so much so that a treatment of each of them as separate entities would be an impossible task.

Membership into the ecclesial community is gained by means of the sacrament of baptism which produces three effects: union of the Christian with Christ, his insertion into the Church and his active participation in the Church's mission. These involve certain demands for the baptized in their common vocation to holiness or to the practice of love of God, as His children, and love of neighbour, as brothers and sisters to each other. The specific identity of the religious life, as a full living of this common vocation, consists then in living in an *intense and radical way* this baptismal call in personal and ecclesial, mystical and apostolic dimensions. This is indeed the meaning of religious consecration. Religious consecration, we have tried to show, far from being only a 'setting apart' for a sacred usage as has been traditionally believed, is equally a deepening of this baptismal consecration. It is a strong desire to add something to the normal demands of Christian life; it is living an 'extra quality' of Christian life and going an extra mile, which quite often goes by the name 'a radical following of Christ'. This desire to do something 'more,' is the reason behind the general understanding of religious life as a life of perfection, that is, a life where one continuously *strives for* and not where one *settles for.* In other words, it means spending one's life trying and struggling relentlessly to do God's will.

The evangelical counsel spells out this 'more' or 'extra quality' of the Christian life. It serves as a catalyst that interiorly transforms the individual through meaning and direction. The vow therefore is both active and dynamic; it is a *process of becoming* poor, chaste and obedient. It is not a state one arrives at on the day of religious profession but a *process* in which one purges one's life of all attachments to things and persons, of self-will so as to become daily what one is not or has not yet fully become. The driving force for this insistent striving is love. That is why each religious vow is an offering of love: *Poverty* is charity which refuses to hoard for oneself and which opens oneself to others in giving to them what one possesses; *Chastity* is charity which refuses to seek pleasure in oneself and in others and puts oneself wholeheartedly at the disposition of others in such a way that everyone can have recourse to one without becoming one's prisoner; *Obedience* is charity which refuses to impose itself and puts all its energies and creativity at the service of the Kingdom of God, thereby establishing a strong relationship with the *persona Christi.*

In order to offer oneself 'more' to God by means of public vows, one needs to attend the school of the Lord's service which is called religious formation. This is a continuous learning process in which one advances unceasingly both in self-knowledge and in the knowledge of God to better serve Him. In view of this, a novice is accompanied progressively in this arduous process of spiritual maturation so as to acquire a particular cultural religious identity. In order to achieve this, there is initial formation which aims at preparing the novice for consecration through the vows. This formation has human, psychological, communal, spiritual, religious, intellectual and apostolic dimensions. In this work we have attempted to delineate areas of concern in this formative process, so that the whole person will be fit for the *total self-giving* which would lead him/her to conform him/herself to Christ (VC 65). Just as the evangelical counsel is *an endless process of becoming* that terminates in death, so is religious formation a *life-long process* of constant search for faithfulness to God and to one's religious consecration. This search equally ends when one dies. Therefore we suggested by way of examples different approaches to continuing formation for the aged members of our congregations especially those who were once very active members. We offered our own reflections on how to help them come to the awareness that advancement in age is not synonymous with loss of relevance. To be at the centre of things is not *only when we give* but also when we *receive*, and those who cannot yet give or those who can no longer give, may yet give, in *receiving* care. By so doing, they make possible a deepening and extension of spirit in the lives of those who care for them and in their communities. Theirs is the gift of being open to caring love, which also is a *process* that has to be learnt.

At the end of the chapter on religious formation we highlighted the fact that religious formation does not necessarily bring about spiritual transformation, but that it instead predisposes one for it. Transformation is primarily attributed to the grace of God coupled with human cooperation.

Fraternal life in common or community life is the ideal ground where the religious carries out the intense search for this continuous Christian quality of life. In it, the religious commits him/herself through his/her vows to a unity that has no natural 'glue' in order to witness to the possibility and reality of the transcendent unity made possible by Christ on the Cross of Calvary. Unity with this group gives him/her a strong sense of belonging. The experience of this unity in the inter-relatedness of the members exposes the religious to an unavoidable vulnerability before one another. As a consequence, the community life of the religious becomes a place of forgiveness par excellence because it is quite often burdened by conflict and thus calls always for reconciliation. Following on this, we can say that the mystery of forgiveness is tangible in a religious community. This forgiveness and reconciliation eventually bring love, peace and joy the moment every member co-operates in adopting the broader perspective of life where the motto is 'me-and-you' and not 'me-or-you'. It is with this understanding that we could justifiably refer to the religious life as the place for 'extra quality' of Christian life and it is within the atmosphere of the community life that the vows are to be faithfully lived.

With the above analysis having been done, we were able to progressively move forward in our search for the *raison d'être* of religious life. Starting from the religious identity of Christ and the Apostles down the centuries we saw that the unique role of the religious in the ecclesial community has never been on the basis of mere functionality. Our analysis led us to understand that there exists always the inherent danger of taking refuge in 'our apostolate' and using it as walls to safeguard our lack of real identity. Without an adequate examination of what constitutes the real identity of the religious, these walls are bound to fall down. Consequently, our research led us into an examination of the unique role of religious life in the Church and we endeavoured to demonstrate that that the distinctive role of the religious in the ecclesial community have always been and therefore should always be:

- *What* and at the same time *who* we are in the Church (RD 15), that is, total dedication and consecration of ourselves to God in our daily and routine lives.
- That this total self-donation or dedication by means of the three vows is made manifest in the religious apostolate which is a concrete way to show or to prove one's love of God in one's Institute. Hence religious consecration and religious apostolate are blended together in a unique identity.
- That the *real apostolate* of a religious is *essentially love* expressed in service to the suffering humanity and compassion to the sinned-against after the example of Christ who is the Ideal of the religious (Luke 4:16-18; Luke 7:22; Matthew 9:36-37).
- That the role of the religious is primarily and essentially *eschatological* because that to which the religious bear witness with their lives is beyond time and space. The baptized bears witness that God is to be loved *in omnibus,* that is, *in all things,* while the religious, '*adding something to this*', says with his/her life that God is also to be loved *super omnia,* that is, *above all things.*
- That the life of the religious is *sacramental,* a

signpost pointing to the Kingdom. It is a sign that with its mere presence evangelizes. The value of religious life is inherent in the life itself; it is a prophetic life-form.

- That the religious is a *proleptic eschatological sign* of the Kingdom of God.
- That all these requisites to religious life are all wrapped, sealed and ratified in and by means of a deep relationship with God in Christ.

Since the religious life constitutes *a living memory of Jesus' way of living and acting* as the Incarnate Word in relation to the Father and in relation to the brethren (VC 22), it becomes self-evident that the motivation for such a life should not be sought on the empirical plane or on the level of usefulness, achievements, purposefulness and still less in cultures. This is often the temptation, especially when one hides under the pretext of rendering it more 'reasonable' and humanly 'attractive', while simultaneously ignoring the risk of emptying it of its meaning and purpose, which paradoxically is purposelessness. To this effect, Pigna Arnaldo has wonderfully observed that:

> The Evangelical counsels are chosen not to attain the fullness of the human values, but to empty oneself as did Christ, and thus to allow love to express itself and reveal itself in a new way. But this is possible only due to the miracle of love itself. This is a

> love which communicates itself and gives one the capacity of doing the same, in arousing a response of which we are radically incapable. It is for this reason that the counsels are gift.[1]

So *the love of Christ* is the only defining motivation that gives meaning and value to the religious life. To understand this love, it is necessary to plunge into its mystery which is essentially *a stripping of the self* and consequently a gift of self (Philippians 2:6-8), rather than a trusting in the logic of reason and of culture, which assign unnecessary values to 'human achievements', thereby turning religious houses into career institutions, with religious apostolate or mission as their brand names. Someone who is aware of having received all, his very being and his life, as gift from God (in the sense that God chooses and consecrates), understands that fidelity to the truth of his own being and *becoming* implies a continual acceptance of himself as gift which surrenders totally to God and generously gives to others. This total surrender is shown in the religious apostolate or Mission, whose characteristic hallmark is service.

The energy and the incentive for such a selfless service is sought in the quiet moments of prayer. Prayer as we have tried to demonstrate is *primus inter pares* among the four pillars of religious life. Intimate union with God in prayer is the source and sustenance of religious life. Sustained by this union with God in prayer, to follow Christ then means: to let go of excessive attachments to passing pleasures and possessions (chastity); to ploys of autonomous power (obedience); to tangible goods as if they were ultimate (poverty). One learns from experience that this programme of ego-stripping is a prescription for more personal wholeness and holiness, for living a balanced life of adoring God's ineffable mystery (*oratio*/contemplation) and thereby exercising compassion for our own and other peoples' wounded condition (action/mission).

Furthermore, the religious live their lives with the consciousness of the fact that today the evangelical counsels and the Gospel values which the religious life is meant to uphold are regarded as foolishness by many. This is why the religious must continually remind and reassure themselves that the counsels manifest God's 'foolishness' (1 Corinthians 1:25-28), and embody the wisdom and power of God. They must bear in mind that God's notion of what is important is different from ours and just as His thoughts are not our thoughts, His ways are equally not our ways (cf. Isaiah 55:8). It must be clear to the religious that it is in such 'foolishness', 'where valiant fools gather to proclaim the outrageous possibility of love and freedom, that the power of salvation can break through, and save even those who least suspect the nature of what is happening to them.'[2] So to answer 'yes' to this 'foolishness' of God, is, at the same time, to answer 'no' to all the rest – the wisdom of the world. When we move beyond a purely logical, rationalistic analysis of the religious life, it then becomes possible for us to understand that a life lived in love and for Love according to the counsels and the Gospel values, has a special role to play in the salvation and the liberation of humanity. This is our hope and our prayer! With this in mind we confidently conclude with the words of Sandra Schneider saying:

> The important thing is not that one spends a whole life doing something but what one does with one's whole life and how one does it. The important thing is not that one does not change one's state of life but that one does change, unceasingly, *so as to be able to grow into the fullness of life that was dimly outlined by the initial promise. It is this fundamental commitment to change and growth* that allows us to see life commitment not as entrapment in static structures but as *ongoing dynamic involvement with the whole of life*, whatever the circumstances may be. (Schneider 1986, 204)[3]

Ut in Omnibus Glorificetur Deus!
Dinklage, Germany.

Notes

1 Pigna ARNALDO, Repartir du Christ. La spiritualité des Voeux. Burtin: Éditions des Béatitudes, 2001, p. 33.

2 Rosemary HAUGHTON, 'Divine Love Breaking through into Human Experience', in: *Cross Currents* 71, No 281, 1982, pp. 20-28, here p. 28.

3 Quoted by D. O'MURCHU, Poverty, Celibacy, and Obedience, pp. 32-33. The emphases are mine.

BIBLIOGRAPHY

ARBUCKLE Gerald, FLEMING David, (eds.), Religious Life. Rebirth Through Conversion, Middle Green, Slough, 1990.

ARNALDO Pigna, Repartir du Christ. La spiritualité des voeux. Burtin: Éditions des Béatitudes, 2001.

BALDUCELLI Roger, O.S.F.S., The Decision for Celibacy, in: Theological Studies 36 No 21, 1975, pp. 219-242.

BAYNHAM B, 'Transformation,' in: M. DOWNEY (ed.), *The New Dictionary of Catholic Spirituality,* Liturgical Press: Collegeville 1993.

BONNIE BOWMAN Thurston, 'Expository Articles Matthew 5:43-48', in: *Interpretation* 41, no 2 April 1987, pp.170-173.

BISIGNANO Sante, 'La formazione permanente: linee fondamentali, criteri itinerari', in: *COLLECTION, La formazione permanente nella vita religiosa* Editrice Rogate: Rome 1984.

'Itinerario di formazione alla vita religiosa', in: *COLLECTION, Vita consacrata un dono del Signore alla sua Chiesa* Elle Di Ci: Leumann Turin, 1994.

BUECHNER Frederick, 'Journey Towards Wholeness', in: *Theology Today* 49, 1993, pp. 454-464.

BUJO Bénézet, Foundations of an African Ethics. Beyond the universal claims of Western Morality, The Cross Road Publishing Company, New York, 2001.

CASEY Michael, 'Compassion: The Mainspring of Ministry', in: *Tjurunga* 38, 1990, pp. 3-12

'Consecrated Chastity: Reflections on the Text of Gertrude of Helfta', in: *Tjurunga* 31, 1986, pp. 3-14.

CASSIEN Jean, Conférences : in Sources Chrétiennes 64, Ed. par. E. PICHERY, Paris 1959, III, pp. 14-16.

CORNELIUS Helena and FAIRE Shoshana, Everyone can win. How to Resolve Conflict, Australia, 1996.

CLARK Ron, 'Family Management or Involvement? Paul's Use of προΐστημι in 1 Timothy 3 as a Requirement for Church Leadership' in: *Stone-Campbell Journal 9*, 2006.

CHINIGO Michael, (ed.,) The Pope Speaks, Pantheon, 1957.

DAMMERTZ Viktor, 'Poverty in the Rule of St Benedict and today', in: *The American Benedictine Review,* 35 1984, pp.1-16.

DANIELOU Jean, Nuns, What is special about them? London, 1974.

DEVOGNE A., « Monachisme et Eglise dans la pensée de Cassien », in : Id., *Téologie de la vie monastique. Etudes sur la tradition patristique*, Cerf, Paris 1961, pp. 213-240.

FARLEY Edward, Ecclesial Man, Philadelphia, 1975.

FIAND Barbara, Living the Vision. Religious Vows in an Age of Change, New York, 1990.

FLANNERY A., (ed.).Religious and Human Advancement, January 1981, No. 7 in Vatican Council II, Vol. 2, p. 267

FLEMING David, 'Understanding a Theology of Religious Life', in: *Religious Life, Rebirth through Conversion*, G.

ARBUCKLE & D. FLEMING (eds.). Middle green, Slough, 1990, pp. 21-79.

FUNG Raymond, 'Compassion for the Sinned-against', in: *Theology Today*, 37 No 2 1980.

GAMBARI E., Religious Life. According to Vatican II and The New Code of Canon Law, St Paul Editions, Boston 1986.

GUIVER George, Pursuing the Mystery. Worship and daily life as Presence of God, SPCK London, 1996.

GUNZEL Raymond J. Celibacy: Renewing the Gift, Releasing the Power. Kansas: Sheed and Ward, 1985.

GRUBER Margareta, KIECHLE Stefan (eds.), Gottes Freundschaft. Ordensleben heute denken, Echter Verlag GmbH, Würzburg, 2007.

HADDAD Frieda, 'Orthodox Spirituality, The Monastic Life', in: *Ecumenical Review 38 No* 1, 1986, pp. 64-70.

HAMER Jean Jérome Card., OP, 'Il Senso Ecclesiale della vita Religiosa al Servizio dell'uomo dell'America Latina', in: *SCRIS* 11, 1985, pp. 57-64

HART Dolores & DENEUT Richard, The Ear of the Heart. An Actress' Journey from Hollywood to Holy Vows, Ignatius Press, San Francisco, 2013.

HAUGHTON Rosemary, 'Formation and Transformation', in: *Conversion: Perspectives on Personal and Social Transformation,* ed. Walter Conn New York: Alba House, 1978.

'Divine Love Breaking through into Human Experience', in: *Cross Currents* 71, No 281, 1982, pp. 20-28.

HERZIG Anneliese, In der Spur Jesu. Leben nach den Evangelischen Räten, Innsbruck-Wien, 2012.

'Lebenskultur nach den evangelischen Räten Antwort – Symbol – Gestaltungsprinzip', in: *Gottes Freundschaft. Ordensleben heute denken,* Margareta Gruber und Stefan Kiechle (eds.), Echter Verlag GmbH, Würzburg, 2007. pp. 72-87.

HODES Aubrey, Encounter with Martin Buber, London, 1972.

John Paul II, Il Religioso testimonia al mondo una vita dedicata tutta a Dio (10-11 Marzo 1986) in: *INFORMATIONES S.C.R.I.S.* XII, n. 1, 1986.

KELLY Edward C.S.S.P, 'The Religious Life and the Apostolate', in: *AFER,* 7 No 3 1965, pp. 215-219.

KNAPP Andreas, Brennender als Feuer. Geistliche Gedichte, Mit einem Essay von Bischof Manfred Scheuer, Echter Verlag GmbH, 2004.

KNIGHT David B., S.J., 'Joy and Judgement in Religious Obedience', in: *Studies in the Spirituality of the Jesuits, Published by the American Assistancy Seminar on Jesuit Spirituality, especially for American Jesuits working out their aggiornamento in thespirit of Vatican Council,* Vol. VI, No. 3, 1974, pp. 131-168.

KIECHLE Stefan, '*Consecratio – Communio – Missio.* Die drei Grundelemente des Ordenslebens', in: Margareta GRUBER, Stefan KIECHLE (edd.), *Gottes Freundschaft. Ordensleben heute denken,* Echter Verlag GmbH, Würzburg, 2007, pp. 51-71.

KRENIK Thomas, Formation for Priestly Celibacy: A Resource Book. Washington: D.C: National Catholic Educational Association, 1999.

LODER James E., 'The Fashioning of Power: A Christian Perspective on the Life-Style Phenomenon', in: A. J. MCKELWAY and E. David WILLIS, eds., *The Context of Contemporary Theology,* Atlanta 1974, pp. 187-205.

The Transforming Moment, San Francisco Harper & Row, 1981.

LOHKAMP N., 'Consecration, Personal', in: *The New Catholic Encyclopedia,* Second Edition 4, Thomas Gale, Washington, D.C., 2003.

LOMBARD Helen, 'The Distinctive Role of Religious', in: *Tjurunga An Australasian Benedictine Review*, 28 1985, pp. 3-13.

LONERGAN Bernard, Method in Theology, New York 1997.

LOTZ Louis E., 'Perplexing text Matthew 5:48', in: *The Reformed Journal*, 29 No 4 April 1979.

MCALPIN K., 'Conversion. A Summons from the Word of God', in: *Review for Religious* 61 2002.

MACKRELL Gerard, Thoughts for Religious, middle green, Slough, 1984.

MANDELA Nelson, The Long Walk to Freedom, London 1994.

MERKLE Judith, A Different Touch: A Study of Vows in Religious Life, Collegeville, Minnesota: The Liturgical Press, 1998.

MEZIROW J., Transformative Dimension of Adult Learning, Jossey- Bass: San Francisco, 1991.

MURNION Philip, 'A Sacramental Church in the Modern World', in: *Origins, N.C. Documentary Service* 14 (6), 1984.

NANNI C., 'Formazione', in J. M. PRELLEZO - C. NANNI - G. MALIZIA (eds.), Dizionario delle Scienze dell'Educazione Elle Di Ci: Leumann Turin, 1997.

NORRIS Kathleen, 'Everyday Mysteries: A Religious Life in the Real World', in: *The Mennonite Quarterly Review* 82, 2008, pp. 7-12.

O'BRIEN M.J. – R.J. STEIMEL, Psychological Aspects of Spiritual Development The Catholic University of America Press: Washington, 1965.

O'DONOHUE John, Eternal Echoes. Exploring our Hunger to Belong. London, 1998.

O'MURCHU Diarmuid, Poverty, Celibacy, and Obedience. A Radical Option For Life, New York, 1999.

Religious Life A Prophetic Vision Notre Dame Indiana: Ave Maria Press, 1995.

PARDILLA Angel, 'Theological Identity of Religious Life', in: INFORMATIONES s.c.r.i.s. (Sacra Congregazione per i Religiosi e gli Istituti Secolari), Anno XII, n. 1 giugno 1986.

PAREDES José Cristo Rey Garcia, „Die Hoffnung als unsere Sendung im europäischen Kontext' (Fortsetzung), in: *OK Ordens-Korrespondenz. Zeitschrift für Fragen des Ordenslebens* 51 (2010), pp. 452-469.

RADCLIFFE Timothy, Sing a New Song: The Christian Vocation, Dominican publications Dublin, 2000.

RAHNER Karl, 'The Lay Apostolate', in: *Cross Currents* 7 No 3 1957

'Reflections on Obedience a basic Ignatian concept', in: *Cross Currents* 10 No 4 1960. pp 363-374.

The Practice of Faith, New York, 1983.

RHYS Ernest, (ed.), 'The Tragedy of King Lear', in: *Poetry and the Drama. Shakespeare's Tragedies*. Everyman's Library, London, 1910.

RONAN J.L., 'World', in: *The New Catholic Encyclopedia,* Second Edition 14, Thomas Gale, Washington, D.C., 2003.

SAUVAGE Michel, Les fondements évangéliques de la vie religieuse, in : *Lassalianum* 16 May 1973, pp. 68-71.

SCHARLEMANN Robert P., The Being of God, New York, 1981.

SCHNEIDER Sandra, 'Evangelical Equality. Religious consecration, Mission and Witness' in: *Spirituality Today* 39/1 (Spring 1987).

'Task of those who choose Prophetic Life style'; the fourth part of a five-part essay on the Meaning of Religious Life Today, in: *National Catholic Reporter. The Independent News Source*, Jan 7 2010.

SENGE Evelyn, Quaker Faith and Practice: The Yearly Meeting of the Religious Society of Friends, London 1999, Personal journey Section 21:45.

SILVAS Anna M., The *Asketikon* of St Basil the Great. (English translation of the Longer Responses and the Shorter Responses), Oxford University Press, 2005.

SIPE A.W. Richard, Celibacy. The Oxford Companion to Christian Thought, Ed. Adrian Hastings New York: Oxford University Press, 2000.

'Celibacy Today. Mystery, Myth and Miasma', in: *Cross Currents* 58 No 4 2008, pp. 545-562.

STEIN M., Transformation. Emergence of the Self , A & M University Press: Laredo, 1998.

SYNDER Ross, 'Religious Meaning and the latter third of Life', in: *Religious Education* 76, 5 1981, pp. 534-552.

TASSOTTI S., La consacrazione religiosa. Dal Concilio Vaticano II all'Esortazione Apostolica *'Vita Consecrata'*, OCD, Città di Castello. 2003.

THOMAS Chris, 'Rediscover your first Love', in: *Good News, Catholic Charismatic Renewal Serving the Church*, No. 190, London July/August 2007.

TILLARD J.-M.R., Davanti a Dio e per il mondo. Il progetto dei religiosi, Paoline, Alba 1975, pp. 108-133.

'Consigli evangelici', in: *Dizionario degli Istituti di Perfezione*, II Paoline, Roma 1975, pp. 1630-1685.

UGORJI Lucius Iwejuru, DMMM at 50. Witnessing to God's Mercy. A Sermon on the occasion of the Golden Jubilee Celebration of the DMMM Sisters, Lumen Press Umuahia, 2011.

Sermon on the Golden Jubilee of a Priest, Port Harcourt, 2013. (unedited work).

VANIER Jean, Community and growth, London, 1979.